GOD IN THE DARK

About the author:

Peter Longson (a pseudonym) is a chamber musician and accompanist who received his education at The Royal Academy of Music and Balliol College, Oxford. He has performed all over the UK and Europe, made seven CDs and has taken part in many live broadcasts and recordings for the BBC. He is now a Professor of Piano, Accompaniment and Vocal Repertoire at one of the UK's music conservatoires.

As a teacher he enjoys the challenge of using words to explain ideas about music, and of guiding the development of talented students. As a writer his aim is to articulate in non-technical language his own difficulties with Christian belief and to help others find a way through their struggles with faith. Though based in theology and philosophy, his writing aims to be accessible and practical, so that it can be of pastoral benefit to his readers.

GOD IN THE DARK

Rebuilding faith when bad stuff happens

Peter Longson

wild goose
publications

www.**iona**books.com

Copyright © 2012 Peter Longson
Every effort has been made to contact the copyright holders of quoted material
for permission and any omissions will be corrected in future edtions.

First published 2012

Wild Goose Publications
4th Floor, Savoy House, 140 Sauchiehall Street, Glasgow G2 3DH, UK
www.ionabooks.com
Wild Goose Publications is the publishing division of the Iona Community.
Scottish Charity No. SC003794. Limited Company Reg. No. SC096243.

ISBN 978-1-84952-215-1

Cover design © Chris Tomlin

The publishers gratefully acknowledge the support of the Drummond Trust,
3 Pitt Terrace, Stirling FK8 2EY in producing this book.

A catalogue record for this book is available from the British Library.

Overseas distribution:
Australia: Willow Connection Pty Ltd, Unit 4A, 3-9 Kenneth Road,
Manly Vale, NSW 2093
New Zealand: Pleroma, Higginson Street, Otane 4170, Central Hawkes Bay
Canada: Novalis/Bayard Publishing & Distribution, 10 Lower Spadina Ave.,
Suite 400, Toronto, Ontario M5V 2Z2

Printed by Martin's the Printers, Berwick upon Tweed

MIX
Paper from
responsible sources
FSC
www.fsc.org   FSC® C013254

CONTENTS

1 **Finding a Voice**
   Who's asking?   8
   Permission to speak   16
   Clearing the decks   29

2 **The Way the World Is**
   A rock and a hard place   40
   Farewell to Pangaea   58
   God of the blank cheque   69

3 **Rogues' Gallery**
   Introduction   92
   The things we say   95
   The devil and all his works   105
      The devil and death   108
      The devil and evil   114
   Bring on the good times   118
      No 'Back to the Future'   118
      Somewhere over the rainbow   123

4 **Finding God in the Dark**
   Made to be makers   134
      God's Symphony   151
   God's music   159
   Praying in the dark: a liturgy   174

For John and Elizabeth, who have walked with us in love

and with grateful thanks to the editor, Sandra Kramer,
for her encouragement, patience and wisdom

One

FINDING A VOICE

WHO'S ASKING?

Into my heart an air that kills
From yon far country blows;
What are those blue remembered hills,
What spires, what farms are those?

That is the land of lost content,
I see it shining plain,
The happy highways where I went
And cannot come again.

(A.E. Housman: *A Shropshire Lad*)[1]

It's gone forever, that funny, young, lost look that I loved. It won't come back again. I killed that too, when I told you about Rebecca ... It's gone, in twenty-four hours. You are so much older ...

(Daphne du Maurier: *Rebecca*)[2]

Most of us are professionals, rather than amateurs, when it comes to the sorrows of the world. Not, of course, in the prosaic sense of making our living from them, but in the deeper sense of being intimately and personally connected to them, of knowing them from the inside. The sorrows of the world have become 'our business'. Many will be able to identify a moment after which 'nothing would ever be the same

---

[1] A.E. Housman, *A Shropshire Lad*, Poem XL, Wordsworth Editions, 1994, p 58

[2] Daphne du Maurier, *Rebecca* (first publ. Victor Gollancz Ltd, 1938), Virago Press, 2003, p 336. Reproduced with permission of Curtis Brown Group Ltd, London on behalf of The Chichester Partnership. Copyright © Daphne du Maurier 1938.

again'. Others will be aware of the slow drip of barely articulated thought that eventually leads to the realisation that, notwithstanding its many glories, the world can be a dark, dangerous and often disappointing place. For the sake of brevity, we will call it for now 'the problem of evil'. This 'evil' can, as we shall soon see, be something for which another human being may be responsible, or it can be the sort where a bad thing 'just happens'. Either way, this experience, and the knowledge it brings, leads us, if we can face it, to one conclusion: we must forever afterwards understand the world and the meaning of our place in it primarily in the light of the bad stuff that happens within it.

Even for those who have not themselves been touched directly in this way, I think it is impossible to live meaningfully in the early 21st century without being aware of 'evil'. Politicians have taken to using the word as a response to horrific world events, or as a description of the soil from which some of those events may have sprung – often using the concept as a justification for taking violent action that in their view 'responds' to it. Tabloid newspapers are quick to brand various types of lawbreakers as 'evil', though their choices of who qualifies are invariably selective. But awareness of evil is not confined to the makers of public opinion: any imaginative engagement with contemporary life will soon put each of us in the shoes of those who have experienced evil at first hand. And in an age whose character is moulded to a greater or lesser degree by radio, television and the internet, we really don't have the option of remaining detached or unaware. Writing with some approval of postmodernity, though with much criticism too, N.T. Wright says that that world-view is 'precisely a restatement of the problem [of evil]';[3] and it is in that post-

---

[3] N.T. Wright, *Evil and the Justice of God*, SPCK, 2006, p 5

modern world that we live, whether we like it or not.

What then are we to do with this knowledge, this experience? For those who have, or had, some kind of Christian faith, I think there are three possibilities. We may decide that God can no longer be trusted, and perhaps that the God we thought we knew was a horrible mistake. We may try to stick it out, holding on to a form of belief that is at odds with our experience of life. Or we may take the most risky and, frankly, the most difficult option: trying to build a Christian understanding that looks the facts full in the face whilst holding on – for dear life – to belief in a God of love.

Later we shall look at those possibilities in more detail. But first, let us identify ourselves, this congregation of the bewildered, this jostling crowd united in some kind of grief, yet each of us separated from all the others by the very uniqueness of our own experience. Many Christians, or would-be Christians, have great difficulty in squaring what we might call 'the facts of life' with what appear to be the confident and neatly packaged truths that are presented as the foundations of Christian belief, and to which once, perhaps, we assented with relative ease – even with joy. Each one's story will be different, but the unifying thread is that of crying 'Why?' 'Why did God allow – that?' 'Why did God not prevent – that?' And then if the 'why' question is entertained, even for a moment, the floodgates open: 'Where was God – then?' 'Can God any longer be relied on?' 'Does prayer get any further than the inside of my head?' 'Is the only answer that God will wipe away all tears – but not yet?' Each individual will have come to these agonies by a different route, but now we find ourselves united in this overwhelming sense of incomprehension. Jürgen Moltmann shines helpful light on what this feels like. 'Anyone who suffers without cause first thinks that he has been forsaken by God.'[4] But, crucially, he continues 'But anyone who cries out to God in this suffering echoes the death-cry of the dying Christ.'[5] It will be some time before we re-establish direct contact with that thought, but it will act as a compass bearing in the journey we are undertaking. It can only be read and entered into correctly, though, if before that we have looked the facts full in the face.

Our particular story can be briefly, though not easily, told, and is best got out of the way here at the start. A daughter who was the victim of a paedophile between the ages of nine and eleven or so. (Unusually, the perpetrator was neither a family member nor someone known to the family.) You don't expect to be taking your young daughter to a clinic for sexually trans-mitted diseases. An all clear verdict didn't improve the situa-tion; it merely meant that things were not even more disastrous than they already were. Then, a couple of years later, as she was beginning to rebuild her life to some kind of normality, a Christian houseparty summer holiday. Doubtless the leaders' prayer that morning was 'Lord, we ask you to pro-tect and be with the young people as they spend the day in the town.' Her day finished with her being raped by one of the other houseparty members. You don't expect to be collecting your daughter's clothes from the police.

As we, each with our own unique story to tell, try to take stock of where we are, a saying of Jesus comes to mind. He had been talking to a young man who afterwards 'went away sad, for he had great wealth'. Jesus comments, 'I tell you the truth, it is hard for a rich man to enter the kingdom of heaven' (Matt 19:22, 23). Clearly, the primary kind of 'rich man' (or woman) he is referring to is one who has a lot of money. But I think we can extend the thought. It was not the money itself that made it so difficult to tune in to Jesus' wavelength: it was the sense of

---

[4] Jürgen Moltmann, *The Crucified God*, SCM Press, 2008, p 261
[5] Ibid., p 261

security that the money produced. 'All's well with the world' is not a cry that will send someone running to God either for comfort or for an explanation of what on earth he thinks he's doing. And frankly, even without our own stories, after the first few years of the much-trumpeted new millennium, it would be a brave soul who was still hanging on to the belief that things are generally pretty much all right in the world at large. But what about one's private, personal world? If there have been no traumas, no bewildering events that make one question God's love or his ability to act, if there has never been that moment of instant and unequivocal knowledge that 'things will never be the same again', then that too is a kind of riches which may make it, in Jesus' language, hard to enter the kingdom of heaven. So it's hard for the wealthy, in whatever sense we care to think of; but it's hard also for those – us – whose faith is teetering on the brink of extinction.

So perhaps we may permit the thought – but *pianissimo* for now, and remembering to come back to it later – that a form of Christian belief that is put together when times are good may have to be abandoned when times go wrong; but that this may be the only route to a properly grown-up faith. This may well involve the pulling down of much that seemed secure and reliable. But, frankly, the demolition has pretty much been done already, and done for us. We are onlookers as faith crumbles. As professionals in the sorrows of life, we are already contemplating the ruins of belief. The stuff that was fine until it wasn't; the image of God that no longer tallies with the facts. It feels like a bereavement. And because of that, I have often found myself half-wishing that I had never known the spurious comfort of a faith that promised so much and apparently delivered so little. It is undoubtedly the case that coming to terms with evil that manifested itself in a pretty brutal form has been made incomparably more difficult by having to place these events in the context of disappointment with God. Disappointment? That's an understatement. But whatever we may call it, the painful truth is that a faith that was supposed to bring comfort brought none at all. In fact it inflicted its own pain, seeming to mock the person who had so cosily believed in a God who could act, and a God who would comfort when things went badly – in short, a God who made a difference.

But, for some reason, the old ingrained habit of wanting to understand everything in the context of faith seems to survive the disaster. It's odd, but I would rather have the difficulty – maybe even the impossibility, who knows? – of trying to rebuild some kind of faith, different though it will be, than abandon God altogether. If I can't make God-sense of all this, then I'm inclined to think that there is no sense to be found. 'We take captive every thought to make it obedient to Christ,' says Paul (2 Cor 10:5). I take that to mean that we may not be wasting our time in trying to find Christ, and a meaning of Christ, in all this dark. And we're not alone: as I said at the beginning, I think there are many who are enduring the apparent poverty of bewilderment, and comparatively few enjoying – except that's not really the right word – the apparent riches of an easy passage through life.

In one way, then, to return to the earlier metaphor, personal disaster, or in our case more accurately family disaster, has been like suddenly being declared bankrupt. I had a faith that belonged to never having faced a major crisis. I thought my 'riches' were a relationship with a loving, forgiving and all-powerful God. (I am a professional classical musician, so serious riches of the financial sort were never likely to feature strongly!) But those riches were gained 'before', when life was relatively plain sailing, and suddenly none of that was any good in the new, unprotected, free-for-all economy of 'after'. Assumptions about God's love, his areas of competence, his ability to make things turn out right, and to answer prayer all suddenly turned out not to be valid currency. There were a lot of bills, and nothing to pay them with.

So it came about that I was already well beyond the age at which one could expect to have got the general hang of 'the world, the universe and everything', when in a matter of minutes all that rather easy certainty was knocked away. To quote another slogan, I thought I had found at least the main answers to 'the meaning of life', the invitation to explore which is the watchword of the popular Alpha course, run by many churches of widely differing colours as an introduction to the Christian faith. I had certainly signed up to its tidy view of how belief in God makes sense of things. The snag is, though, that this tidiness is achieved at some risk of leaving out the difficult stuff that actually happens to people. If 'evil' is confined to the concept of personal guilt, removed by Christ's sacrifice, then however important that may be, we will not have seen the whole picture. I want to come to terms with the mess that isn't my fault.

I could put the situation in the following way; it may be controversial, but it feels inescapable to someone struggling with the aftermath of 'events'. It seems to me that an acknowledgement of personal guilt is by no means necessarily the best, or only, place to start in a search for God. We must look for God first in whatever it is that most perplexes us, whatever it is that lies closest in our field of view. For many, myself included, that will be in the mess of life: the stuff that went wrong, the prayer that wasn't answered, the event that knocked away the certainties of 'life before'. Indeed, we can put this thought more strongly: we *must* look for God in the very place where he is apparently absent. If we think we have found him anywhere else, then he will continue to be absent from that part of our lives that most needs to be healed, and that most needs an explanation.

Well, that was just our story, and I have included it here only to identify myself as one of the bewildered. The details of your story will be utterly different, of course, and perhaps known only to you. It would be impossible to try to categorise all the kinds of grief and disaster, and all the bewildering events, that might cause someone to doubt the God of their former life, and there is no need to. Yours is yours, and mine is mine. But they both exist within the only world we know. In the next chapter we will think about the nature of the world and the way death and disaster seem to be 'built in'. But, to begin with, our task is simply to set out what we are trying to do. This is no less than finding a way of expressing, and living, a Christian world-view that takes as its starting point the bad stuff that happens to people. This is what we must do if we are to have any hope of finding what I would call an honest Christian perspective.

PERMISSION TO SPEAK

There would be no harm, [Alice] thought, in asking if the game was over. 'Please, would you tell me –' she began, looking timidly at the Red Queen. 'Speak when you're spoken to!' the Queen sharply interrupted her. 'But if everybody obeyed that rule,' said Alice, who was always ready for a little argument, 'and if you only spoke when you were spoken to, and the other person always waited for you to begin, you see nobody would ever say anything, so that –' ' Ridiculous!' cried the Queen.

(Lewis Carroll: *Alice's Adventures in Wonderland*, Chapter 9)[6]

What I have just outlined as our goal for this book is admittedly a major task, and not one to be undertaken lightly or unadvisedly, to adapt a thought from the old marriage service. Disturbingly, though, it is apparently also rather a controversial idea. There seems to be, amongst some Christian writing and comment, the idea that this is forbidden territory, or at least that it's akin to the marking on ancient maps that warns 'here be dragons'.

But let's not be too cavalier – perhaps the Bible itself warns us off? 'Such knowledge is too wonderful for me, too lofty for me to attain' (Ps 139:6). But there the poet-writer is referring to the fact that God knows everything about him, and that as humans – the creatures of a creator – we are excluded from that level of all-encompassing knowledge. He is not saying that we may not search: rather that there are finite limits to how far we can get.

Another passage that might at first glance look like a warning against looking for answers is found in Genesis

---

[6] Lewis Carroll, *Alice's Adventures in Wonderland*, first publ. 1865

Chapter 3. The serpent contradicts God's prohibition of eating the fruit of 'the tree of the knowledge of good and evil'. 'You will not surely die,' he says (v. 4 & 5), 'for God knows that when you eat of it your eyes will be opened, and you will be like God, knowing good and evil.' In the next verses we see that this promise was only half true, and that acting on it left a very bitter taste indeed. This myth, in all its artful simplicity, tells us that we are all guilty of making a bid for moral independence, and that the consequence is a sense of alienation from the 'ground of our being'. What it emphatically does not tell us, though, is that we are not to seek understanding of every kind. If being made in the image of God means anything, it must include our love of knowing, and our need to understand.

***

We need to take a brief diversion here, which will be important for understanding what means we have at our disposal for our quest. In referring to Genesis 3, I used the word 'myth' advisedly, in its proper and original sense. In the Introduction to her book *The Battle for God*,[7] Karen Armstrong gives a fine exposition of the correct sense of the concept, which in careless modern usage often doubles as something like 'a widely but thoughtlessly held view, now shown to be false (usually by science)'. She says, 'We tend to assume that the people of the past were (more or less) like us, but in fact their spiritual lives were rather different. In particular, they evolved two ways of thinking, speaking, and acquiring knowledge, which scholars have called *mythos* and *logos* … Myth was not concerned with

---

[7] From *The Battle for God* by Karen Armstrong, Harper Perennial, 2004. Copyright © Karen Armstrong 2000, p xiii ff. Reproduced by permission of the author.

practical matters, but with meaning ... The various mytho-
logical stories, which were not intended to be taken literally,
were an ancient form of psychology ... Because of the dearth of
myth in our modern society, we have had to evolve the science
of psychoanalysis to help us deal with our inner world ...
Logos was equally important. [It] was the rational, pragmatic,
and scientific thought that enabled men and women to function well in the world ... *Logos* forges ahead and tries to find
something new: to elaborate on old insights, achieve greater
control over our environment, discover something fresh, and
invent something novel ... *Logos* had its limitations too. It
could not assuage human pain and sorrow. Rational arguments
could make no sense of tragedy.'

This is very helpful. In our quest to make Christian sense of
tragedy and disaster, we will need to come at it from both these
angles. We need the kind of insights that draw on millennia of
wisdom, coming from the heart to minister to the heart; and
we need also clear-headed courage and clarity of mind to look
the facts directly in the face and work out where to go. The
need for this kind of balance is explained beautifully in the
preface to W.H. Vanstone's book *The Stature of Waiting*.[8]
Acknowledging this as an idea from Paul Tillich, he says:
'(This) method of correlation ... implies that there is a dialec-
tical relationship between divine revelation and human perception: that what we are "told" in revelation is only understood
in the light of our perception of the world around us, while at
the same time our perception of the world around us is itself
illuminated by the light of revelation.' That is a fine and wise
ideal to keep before us.

---

[8] Taken from W.H. Vanstone *The Stature of Waiting* published and copyright 1982 by Darton, Longman and Todd Ltd, London, and used by permission of the publishers.

***

With this in mind, we can return to the business of establishing permission, so to speak, for enquiring into these mysteries. Every parent will know that all children go through a 'why?' phase. Each patient answer to that question only provokes another 'why?' It's rather like those mirrors set up so that you see an infinite number of ever-receding images of yourself, fading away into the distance. Eventually even the most equable parent has to say, 'Well it just is,' and hope that that day's quiz has come to an end. But, however frustrating it is at the time, we know that this obsession with understanding reasons marks, along with the acquisition of language, one of the most important periods of a child's development. If we didn't want to know why, we would remain not in blissful ignorance but in a kind of pathological underdevelopment. And this failure to know would present all kinds of dangers to life and growth, to security and of course to maturity. So wanting to know why is part of being fully human, and for those of us who have very good reason to ask God 'why?' it is crucial for the maturity of our relationship with him.

But there's another snag: as well as the *'forbidden territory'* prohibition, there is also the *'meaningless question'* accusation. Walter Wink has written a horizon-expanding book called *Engaging the Powers*. 'My thesis,' he writes, 'is that what people in the world of the Bible experienced and called "Principalities and Powers" was in fact real.' His assertion that 'The Powers are good, The Powers are fallen, The Powers must be redeemed' is a helpful context in which to set out on our journey. But he also says, 'I have long been struck by the virtual absence of any attempt to explain evil (theodicy) in the New Testament' and 'The early Christians *expected* to be assaulted by the Powers. Never once do they seem puzzled by this fact. It would have been unthinkable for them to ask, "Why do bad things happen to good people?" "[9]

This I think we can perhaps understand and accept in relation to persecution for one's faith – the early Church certainly needed a day-by-day reference point for that experience. But by no means all the bad things that happen to good people are because of someone's, or the Powers', opposition to their Christian faith. Bad things happen *despite* their faith, as well as because of it, and for those who had faith and now are not sure, that is the heart of the problem. Are we to suppose that, back in New Testament times, the mothers of the children murdered by Herod's henchmen in the Massacre of the Innocents did not cry out to God, 'Why *my* son?' and 'Why did we ever come to Bethlehem?' and 'Can God possibly love us if this is how he shows it?'? I am quite sure they did.

Incidentally, in recounting this horrific story Matthew gives an important role to Joseph. As head of the household, it is he who receives special warning about Herod's murderous intentions, and so is able to take the family as refugees to Egypt. This raises a question and a problem. We must phrase it gently, and with due respect – but was the life of each boy killed less precious to his parents than that of the child who was saved by special God-initiated intervention? I think not. So although we cannot know all the detail of the how and the why of the survival of Jesus into adulthood, this story illustrates in a disturbing way what at least appears to us – who are, so to speak, two-dimensional creatures dealing with a multidimensional God – to be the inescapable element of randomness in the way the bad stuff is parcelled out. And now in our own day we each have our own story to tell, though for some that story may

---

[9] Walter Wink, *Engaging the Powers*, Fortress Press, 1992, pp 6, 10, 314ff

have to remain the very private territory of a few trusted friends. But we have to understand, and we have to take the risk of wanting to understand.

John Polkinghorne puts the problem honestly in *The Way the World Is*: 'I believe that this problem of theodicy, of understanding God's ways in the light of the mixture of goodness and terror which we find in the world, constitutes the greatest difficulty that people have in accepting a theistic view of reality. For those of us who stand within the Christian tradition, it remains a deep and disturbing mystery, nagging within us, of which we can never be unaware.'[10] This book is an attempt to listen to that nagging voice, and to seek a Christian perspective as we follow where it leads.

Finally there is one more possible argument to consider that might be raised against our undertaking. We could call it the '*all sewn up*' assertion. This would say that everything we need for salvation and the knowledge of God has been delivered 'once and for all'. For instance, in the doxology at the very end of Romans, Paul speaks of the 'revelation of the mystery hidden for long ages past, but now revealed and made known ...' (Rom 16:25, 26). And while we are on the subject of the last sentences of books, we might also notice the scary imprecation at the end of the Book of Revelation: 'I warn everyone who hears the words of the prophecy of this book: If anyone adds anything to them, God will add to him the plagues described in this book' (Rev 22:18). This has for me the flavour of a quarantining of the strange ideas contained in the Book of Revelation – so that whatever message St John may have for us in the 21st century, it does not confer on us the right to view contemporary events in the same apocalyptic

---

[10] John Polkinghorne, *The Way the World Is*, first publ. Triangle, 1983. 1994 ed. Triangle SPCK, p 21

terms. Incidentally this might be a useful counterbalance to some of the religious response, especially from the United States, to the dangerous times in which we live.

But to return to the idea that everything we need for salvation has been given to us, so we should not add to it: well – yes and no. Yes, in the sense that historically the Jewish preparation for the coming of Jesus, as Christians would see it, has happened; and the events of his life, death, resurrection and ascension have happened. The Christian faith is a story, or it is nothing. But I am sure that each generation must interpret that story, and embed it in its own time, and in the concerns of its own time. An example or two may help. It took three centuries and a doubtless hot debate at the first Council of Nicea (325) to come up with a Trinitarian formulation that we now accept as being quintessentially 'Christian'. This, after the latest books of the Bible were written not later than about 120, with the first list of Christian writing dating to around 170, and the first reference to the New Testament as we now have it being as late as 367.[11] It took time to understand the implications revealed by the biblical narrative for the way in which we might speak of God as 'person'.

Or again: it took a shameful eighteen centuries for the church to realise that slavery was a denial of the uniqueness and infinite value to God of the individual. The criticism that Paul endorsed slavery (the twice-repeated 'Slaves, obey your earthly masters', Eph 6:5 and Col 3:22) is careless. This was about how to live beautifully in hard circumstances. The movement for the abolition of slavery had its roots in the evangelical wing of the church, as well as amongst the Society of Friends, and was a new understanding both of the all-

---

[11] For more on this, see Hilary Brand, *The Sceptic's Guide to Reading the Bible*, Bible Reading Fellowship, 2000, p 47 and elsewhere

embracing life of Christ and of Paul's assertion that we are all one in him. That truth was there, waiting to be found.

Or, nearer to our own time: the glorious dismantling of apartheid had many of its roots in the vision of a latter-day prophet, Archbishop Desmond Tutu, who was able to make a connection between the Christ of the New Testament and the suffering of a people rejected by the ruling race. It's fascinating that some of the imagery from that time is of a black Christ. Well, maybe he was, maybe he wasn't – but that is not the point. His incarnation amongst the victims of apartheid was as one of them, a black Christ. This was a new understanding, specific to the needs and aspirations of the black community.

And so our quest is to find what Christ means for the wounded and the disappointed and the bewildered. To find some new facet of what Paul calls 'the unsearchable riches of Christ' (Eph 3:8). It is as if we are trying to find a new depth of colour amongst the reflective faces of a precious stone. Perhaps now we can move on, believing that what we are doing is both permitted, and that it means something.

But we'd better be honest: this is also a dangerous undertaking. To risk asking questions that theologians and philosophers have been asking since humans began wondering about God and the world and humanity's place in it is to risk losing everything. We might lose even the few shreds of faith that are left. Is it not better to stop asking, cut our losses and wait for heaven? But if we are honest, we realise that we need to know now. We need to look now into the abyss of shattered belief.

One of Jesus' aphorisms on the 'kingdom of heaven' pictures 'a merchant looking for fine pearls' (Matt 13:45). 'When he found one of great value, he went away and sold everything he had and bought it.' Our situation is less certain, and more desperate. We thought we had found the fine pearl, but we are now doubting its provenance. If we have discovered that it is not what we thought, will we find another, the real one that lives up to our needs and expectations? The only way to find that, if it can be found, is to risk selling everything. At this point we cannot know whether this will turn out to have been a successful move. We might finish up with nothing. But then again we just might find what our hearts and minds need.

Investment advisors categorise their clients according to whether they are more or less 'risk-averse'. 'Be aware that the value of your investment may go up or down,' they say – in part of course to avoid the risk for themselves of being accused of mis-selling. I suppose in their own professional lives financial advisors are risk-averse! But we cannot afford to be risk-averse when it comes to looking for God in the dark. We may – in fact we surely will – end our lives still looking, but at least we can say we tried.

There is a very strange story in Genesis (Chapter 32:22 ff) relating how God changes Jacob's name. Because of the circumstances of his birth, he had been given this name which meant something like 'the deceiver'. After a number of visionary experiences of the presence of God, he is on his way to a meeting with his brother Esau, in order to try to bury the hatchet and repair the relationship. 'Jacob was left alone, and a man wrestled with him till daybreak.' This is deeply mysterious, but it seems that in some way it was another meeting with God. For us, who have experienced the overwhelming loneliness and sense of separation that comes with grief, it is hugely significant that as he met with God in this dangerous way, he was completely alone. And dangerous it was. He was fighting God – and winning! But he paid the price in the shape of a God-induced injury to his hip, and thereafter had a limp to show for his trouble. He demanded a blessing, and got a change of name, from Jacob to Israel, meaning 'he struggles with God'. That is a very good description of what we are doing in asking these difficult questions. We may well pick up a wound for our trouble – but we are wounded already, so that won't weigh too heavily. And, like Israel, we might just be able to say, 'I saw God face to face, and yet my life was spared.'

But if it's dangerous, it's also the one thing that's worth doing. For those who have come up short against the dark face of the universe, it's the only thing to do. Unless we want to stay rooted to the spot, we must make this move, and begin this journey, whose destination we cannot know. But if there is a destination at all, it will be the place where tears can begin to be wiped away. And perhaps, too, there may be healing in the journey itself. I freely acknowledge the value for me of making myself write down my thoughts. It brings a kind of control, partial and fitful though it is, over the otherwise impossibly chaotic noise of thoughts and emotions that seem to have a life of their own in the head and the heart.

Doubtless the process of healing and understanding will not be completed in this life, and indeed it would be surprising if there were an instant cure in the next. When the writer of Revelation says that 'God will wipe away every tear from their eyes' (Rev 7:17), he implies perhaps that tears will still be there to be wiped away, or at the very least that the memory of tears will still be sharp. (We will revisit that thought in a slightly different context in a later chapter, Bring on the good times). Yet as we take a deep breath at the beginning of this dangerous but unavoidable journey, is there not a kind of excitement in the air? In my professional life I know what it feels like to begin studying a new work that I will be performing. It can often be a daunting prospect: it may be technically near the limit of my skill, or it may be clear early on that the musical content will be very difficult to make meaningful to the listener. But there is also the prospect of getting inside the mind and heart of the composer, and then in performance being the intermediary between him or her and the listening public. That makes the hard slog of practice bearable. It's just possible, in spite of the difficult terrain we shall be covering, that we may on this journey find our hearts strangely warmed, and our minds strangely stimulated. At least we have each other for company.

There's a beautifully observed moment in Julian Barnes' novel *Flaubert's Parrot*[12], which expresses just why this search is so important. The narrator, Geoffrey Braithwaite, is speaking of Ellen, his former wife. 'She was fond of me – she would automatically agree, as if the matter weren't worth discussing, that she loved me – but she unquestioningly believed the best about me. That's the difference. She didn't ever search for that sliding panel which opens the secret chamber of the heart, the chamber where memory and corpses are kept. Sometimes you find the panel, but it doesn't open; sometimes it opens, and your gaze meets nothing but a mouse skeleton. But at least you've looked. That's the real distinction between people: not between those who have secrets and those who don't, but between those who want to know everything and those who don't. This search is a sign of love, I maintain.' In our life-and-death dispute with God (for that is what it is), all our searching, all our insistence on 'knowing everything', even all our anger with him – all this is a sign of love, I maintain.

***

Finally, there is one more element in this undertaking that we need to acknowledge. As we saw earlier, we need to use our minds as well as our hearts, but we must be aware of the danger

---

[12] From *Flaubert's Parrot* by Julian Barnes, published by Jonathan Cape, 1984. Reprinted by permission of The Random House Group Ltd.

of too much theorising. C.S. Lewis's *The Problem of Pain*[13] is a classic amongst Christian literature on the subject. But it is clearly the work of an academic who at that point, and for a while beyond, had had what we might think of as a comfortable life. Pain may indeed be 'God's megaphone', as he put it, but he could also write that 'if the world is indeed "a vale of soul-making" it seems on the whole to be doing a good job.' Perhaps; but well argued though the book is, this does not, for me at least, have the authentic ring of insider knowledge. The professional theologian, certainly; but not necessarily the 'professional' as regards the sorrows of the world that we thought about as we began. Fast forward to 1960, a few weeks or months after the death of his wife Joy. 'For the first time I have looked back and read these notes,' he began in a third notebook. 'They appal me. From the way I've been talking, anyone would think that Joy's death mattered chiefly for its effect on myself. Her point of view seems to have dropped out of sight. Have I forgotten the moment of bitterness when she cried out, "And there was so much to live for"? ... Is it rational to believe in a bad God? Anyway, in a God so bad as all that? The cosmic sadist, the spiteful imbecile?...'[14] That's more like it. His notebooks became the short but painfully honest book *A Grief Observed*,[15] in which he comes close to losing faith in the God whom he had helped so many to engage with. Hanging on to God by his fingernails when all was lost and every certainty was removed, he had more to say to those in despair than he ever

[13] *The Problem of Pain* by C.S. Lewis copyright © C.S. Lewis Pte Ltd. 1940. Extracts reprinted by permission.

[14] Extract taken from C.S. Lewis: *The Authentic Voice* by William Griffin, published by Lion Hudson plc 1988. Used with permission of Lion Hudson plc.

[15] C.S. Lewis, *A Grief Observed*, Faber and Faber, 1976.

did from the safety of his pre-marriage Oxford don's rooms.

So cool theorising will not do. And yet we have to think it out. I will have more to say later about what art in general, and music in particular, may be able to tell us. It can certainly help us to express, and thereby come to terms with, our emotions – and it's our emotions that take over in those days and weeks and more after the moment we know that nothing will ever be the same again. This is right, and psychologically healthy. But sooner or later we begin to realise – to know in our *minds* – that there are huge consequences for belief and for the way we see the world. And so we have to think our way out. In a book to whose main subject I shall return later, Gregory A. Boyd puts it like this: 'Though some people are more intellectually driven than others, all of us are created to have our minds and our hearts work in sync with each other. Striving to have a plausible theology is necessary because, for many of us, the mind must be thoroughly convinced if the heart is to be thoroughly transformed.'[16] Or, as I would put it, especially in the context of our particular subject: the only way to heal the heart seems to be to seek understanding with the mind. Prayerfully, doubtless. But of course there's a snag even there. Are we praying to the old God? But haven't we just discovered that he didn't do such a good job?

So: 'If you can, help me to think straight' would be a good enough prayer for now.

---

[16] Gregory A. Boyd, *God of the Possible*, Baker Books, 2000, p 90

CLEARING THE DECKS

The unexamined life is not worth living.

(Socrates)[17]

'*Tis better to have loved and lost*
Than never to have loved at all.

(Tennyson)[18]

B efore we go any further, I think I should issue a disclaimer, and then give a brief answer to the potential charge of being a miserable so-and-so. The disclaimer first.

In this book I will be quoting from the writings of a number of theologians and pastors, and usually that will be with grateful approval. Their work and their insights, drawn from lives dedicated to theology and pastoral concern, have helped me as I try to make Christian sense of a confusing and contradictory world. I will also be drawing on the wisdom of some philosophers, scientists and other writers whose work I have found helpful. And yet, and yet … they can only give us pointers; no one but me has my view, my angle, on 'the problem of evil', and no one but you has yours. Most of us do not think of ourselves as theologians or philosophers, but it seems to me that in some ways, to get through life, we need to behave as if we were. The insights of those who are able to spend their lives thinking about these things are always likely to be valuable; but you and I, who are busy just managing from

---

[17] Quoted by Plato in *Apology*. Available in *Plato in 12 Volumes*, Vol. 1, William Heinemann Ltd, 1966.
[18] Alfred, Lord Tennyson, *In Memoriam A.H.H.*, 1849. From Canto 27.

one day to the next, we are the ones whose lives become out-of-the-ordinary when disaster strikes, and we are the ones who must find our own ways of coming to terms with what faith can possibly mean when the unthinkable has happened.

So whatever help there may be from books, and whatever inspiring sermons we may be able to hear, and indeed whatever help we may receive from trusted friends, ultimately we're on our own. This is between me and the God I thought I could rely on. So I'd better face the question: what use is yet another book? And particularly this one, which I am writing in the first instance for myself, in order to slay my own demons, and to try to impose some kind of order on chaos? Well, I don't know how you feel, though I can guess, and I certainly don't know the details. But it's just possible that there's enough common ground to make it worthwhile recording the story of my own search. There will be a lot of blanks that will need filling in, and our paths may not coincide perfectly at every step, but what we have in common is the sharing of an experience which makes it hard, oh so hard, to believe any more in a God of love.

I am convinced that it must be possible, without being trained as a theologian or a philosopher, to think in a Christian way about what I am sure is for many people the greatest stumbling block to faith. Our qualification is not on paper, but is our own experience of a 'before' and an 'after' – the transition, either instantaneous or imperceptible, from untroubled faith to bewildered uncertainty. Christian theology cannot be the exclusive province of theologians, and Christian philosophy cannot be the exclusive province of philosophers. Nor should Christian theology and philosophy inhabit separate worlds. We must take what help we can from the wise, but it is our own experience of being in the middle of the mess of life that is our starting point. Trying to make Christian sense of the mess is always going to be a minority sport, however much one might wish it otherwise, but for those who know they need to engage in it, it feels like the only thing that matters.

I had the huge privilege and good fortune to study the piano with one of the truly great teachers, Gordon Green. He was both inspiring and self-effacing, and brought out the best in his students by making us want to play, and by encouraging us to find our own solutions to musical and technical problems. He was thus the opposite of the many teachers who instil fear in their students, and who obtain quick results by getting them to copy how they play. As a result, there was no identifiable 'house style' amongst his students as we went on to pursue professional careers. Though he was reluctant to speak about himself, I once managed, when I was one of his more senior students, to ask him about his way of teaching. His reply has stayed with me over the years, and although he was not a Christian believer, it has always struck me as a brilliant expression of incarnational thinking. 'Some teachers,' he said, 'say "Come over here and I will show you the way to go". I however go to where the student is, and we make the journey together. The difference between us is just that I have more experience.'

In my own teaching I do my best to follow that high and glorious example, and know how hard that is. We will, I think, return to this incarnational idea much later on, but for now I mention this story for a different reason. It illustrates a kind of deference and an unwillingness to lay down the law too exactly. Someone else may well have some better insight, some clearer vision, and in fact much of what we must find we must find for ourselves. It was in this spirit that Gordon Green once said these parting words to an overseas student at the end of a few years' study with him: 'Go home to your country and forget everything I told you.' If only we could all be so self-forgetful! This is humility, the genuine article, though of course we all remembered, without even trying to, everything he so memorably said.

I hope what I am writing will be understood in something of the same spirit, and I counsel a similarly reticent attitude to what I have to say. These are the thoughts of one Christian, who has found his faith rocked by events. I have no quick solutions, and will pose far more questions than I will offer answers. But it may be that the sharing of this experience may encourage other 'battered Christians' to find their own ways of rebuilding some kind of faith. I offer not the fruit of formal study, and certainly not someone else's 'solution'. Rather, these are my own stumbling attempts to find a Christian way of thinking about a dark world, and of living with my own experience of it.

This mention of experience raises another question which we need to be clear about as we get going, and which at first sight might look like another potential prohibition of the kind we considered in the previous chapter. Am I making my experience – or ours, or yours – the arbiter of what I decide to believe? The post-modern fashion says that the individual and his or her experience is indeed the only justification needed for holding a particular belief. 'If it's true for me, it's true' is the mantra. But I'm afraid that won't do. What we're trying to do here is to find a way of maintaining – or, rather, rebuilding – Christian belief; that can't be just a free-for-all, taking the comfortable bits and ditching the tricky stuff. And, as I've said already, it's being unable to escape from wanting a Christian answer that makes it so painful. But, as Peter said to Jesus (Jn 6:68), where else can we go? Somehow, our job is to understand the Bible, and to rediscover the God of the Bible, in the context of events that have shaken our faith to its foundations.

In his book *The Last Word*, N.T. Wright, the former Bishop of Durham, makes clear the different roles played by the familiar trio of scripture, tradition and reason (with an important caveat about what we mean by reason). But, he says, 'experience' is different. 'It is precisely because "experience" is fluid and puzzling, and because all human beings including devout Christians are prey to serious and multilayered self deception, including in their traditions and their reasoning, ... that "authority" [of God at work through scripture] is needed in the first place.'[19] A timely corrective, to be sure. But it is exactly our experience that has brought us to this point, and we cannot pretend it away. So it's helpful that later he says, 'The positive force of the appeal to "experience" is much better expressed in terms of the *context within which* we hear scripture. Experience, as the necessary subjective pole of all knowing, is the place where we stand as we hear God's word, know his love, and understand his wisdom.' We cannot be anywhere other than where we are, and the place where we stand is the place that our experience has brought us to.

***

But is all this just the point of view of someone whose makeup and character led him to focus on the darkness of the world? Am I, as I wondered at the beginning of this chapter, just a miserable so-and-so? To put it fairly brutally, is all this more about me and my psychology than about some objective picture of God and his world? We will come in due course to a consideration of an idea, widely held amongst Christians I think, though rarely stated explicitly: the idea that yes, there's bad, but yes, there's also good, and that because God is on the side of the good – or even just because there will turn out to be

---

[19] N.T. Wright, *The Last Word*, HarperSanFrancisco, 2005, p 102, 103, 104. By permission of HarperCollins Publishers. In UK *Scripture and the Authority of God*, SPCK, 2005.

more of it! – in the end it will 'win'; and therefore the bad should always be viewed in the light of the soon-to-triumph good. We'll have to be patient and put that somewhere further down the agenda for now. But at this point let's be clear about one thing: if in a 'God's world' there is evil, or bad stuff, or disaster, or grief, or whatever we want to call it, then it's *that* that we are going to have to explain and come to terms with. If it's a God's world then you'd expect it to be full of good and wonderful things. And it is! And we'll make sure that we don't lose sight of them in this exploration. But it's not they that are the problem. This is about theodicy – the word coined by the philosopher Leibniz to stand for the attempt to reconcile the idea of a good God with the fact of evil.

But, and I'd better be honest, there are dangers in approaching this huge and intractable subject from the angle of my, and my family's, personal experience of a particular manifestation of evil. There are certainly two dangers, and maybe more that I cannot see. The first is of portraying myself as the victim. The events that have led me to these thoughts and to this quest – it feels more like a compulsion – to understand the ways of God, did not happen to me, but to my daughter. It is she who must be supported, loved and healed. But we live in families and wider groupings. John Donne was right to say that 'no man is an island', and Margaret Thatcher was dismally wrong in her claim that 'there is no such thing as society'. So there are aspects of all this that affect the rest of us as parents, siblings, the church and the wider society in which bad things happen. From within these different groups I think I have the right to say something as a father who, however feebly, was attempting to place the family within the orbit of God's love and protection. (Note the past continuous tense.)

In a television documentary, the mother of a young man with Tourette's syndrome said, 'I don't know where he ends and I begin.' This artless phrase, spoken unprepared to camera, expresses better than any thought-out statement could do just how close a parent is – there is no choice – to a child's tragedy. I am often painfully aware of the extent to which aspects of my own well-being, if one may put it like that, have become linked to the well-being of the child – now a young adult – whose experiences are the starting point for all this soul-searching. Any parent is of course to a greater or lesser extent defined and remade by the life of his or her children, and I am full of joy and wonder to be intimately and irrevocably caught up with the lives of my children and grandchildren – and now even of 'extra' fostered grandchildren. This is a joy, a blessing and a privilege, and a school for life skills that has lifelong membership. My own closeness to the experience of one child implies no lesser involvement with the lives of the others – this is an additional form of connection rather than a more intense version of what is the case with the others. And in some ways, because its source is things that one would so much wish had never happened, this connection is not something that anyone in his right mind would go looking for. It sometimes feels, even at the distance of a few years, as if parts of her life and mine have been fused together under the white heat of trauma. But it also goes without saying that I am not the only one affected. Each has dealt with it privately in his or her own way, but we have also all shared this together, and supported each other together. Indeed it is clear that in many ways siblings have been able to be more use to each other than their parents could ever be. For such graces, and for the mutuality of their love and support, all of us will always be thankful.

The other danger concerns skewing the whole enterprise under the tug of my own particular psychological make-up. A trusted friend once described, only half-playfully, my 'exceptional ability to see the dark side of life'. Perhaps this has led to a dangerously close imaginative connection to events in the past. Many well-built walls and structures came crashing down in those early days and weeks. But there are also vivid and continuing seismic aftershocks, often unsettling in their insistence. It is probably not irrelevant that this is being written by a professional musician. To be emotionally alert is part of what I am. A musician deals with emotion as his basic diet, or the material he is given to work with, and often that emotion is of the very deepest kind. My own specialism as an accompanist involves a high level of empathy with other performers. On a good day, I can sense when a singer is going to breathe, or how confident they are feeling, or at what emotional level they are functioning, and how to bring the best out of them. And it's two-way traffic: I can transmit emotional and technical signals about how I am feeling, either about the way the performance is going, or what we need to do in that moment to make the performance come alive. This is all good, and in one way is no more than the basic equipment of a musician. But it requires a certain personality type, and a well-developed ability to get inside someone else's head, which cannot be switched on and off in order to function only as a professional tool. It appears unbidden in 'real' life, for better or worse.

But that's just how it is, and I'm not interested in looking for a faith that 'works' only when a psychologist has sorted me out. My 'new' faith, whatever it will be, must be for me now, as I am, 'ability to see the dark side' and all. If God wishes to change my character and my way of seeing the world, then that's fine, but that cannot be the prelude to finding faith. Think of the many people whose lives were changed by meeting Jesus. He spoke with them, or healed them, or invited them to follow him, *as they were.* Change of lifestyle or direction might come later, flowing as a consequence of a new relationship. But their encounter with him was as the 'original' people that they were. So my quest is to find a faith that can meet and encompass both the given of history and experience, and the given of my own personality.

***

To sum up a chapter that I hope has not been too apologetic: first, I am no expert in theology, but, with the help of many who are, I hope to be able to say something that comes from personal experience; and second, whatever may be the details of my own character, I am clear that they do not rule me out from looking long and hard at the nature of the world, and how we may be able to understand and know the God who made and sustains it.

So now it's time to stand well back from the specifics of our own particular story, whatever they may be, and try to get some perspective on the general nature of the created world. First, we'll try to do a bit of 'popular science' and then, in the following chapter, begin to think about the fact that the possibility of 'physical' disaster seems to be built into the system.

Two

THE WAY THE WORLD IS

A Rock and a Hard Place

The applause for the Big Bang was heard only fifteen billion years after the explosion.

Nothing is more surprising than that there's a world at all. We're alive, Vera! It's unbelievable!... I think the universe is intentional.

(Jostein Gaarder: *Maya*)[20]

Let's start with the easy bit. This rock which is the earth is a hard place: that much is obvious. It's also impenetrably old. Some friends of ours have a cottage on the shore of Loch Torridon on the west coast of Scotland, and generously let my wife and me use it for holidays from time to time. The landscape is awe-inspiring, even if in summer we see it through a haze of midges which seem to be positively attracted by the anti-midge cream we have plastered on. Richard Fortey has written an impressive survey of the earth's geology called *The Earth: an Intimate History*.[21] Describing the ancient geology of this beautiful part of the world, he says 'We are looking so far back in time that ghosts and chemistry are our best informants.' And later, 'On Loch Maree we observe that the Torridonian beds fill in the valleys in the original Lewisian surface; they are spread over an older landscape, as a builder might level irregular ground before commencing construction. The ancient surface is being exhumed as erosion, slowly, very slowly, strips away

[20] Jostein Gaarder, *Maya*, Phoenix, 2000. Paperback 2001, p 128, 278

[21] Richard Fortey, *The Earth: an Intimate History*, Harper Perennial, 2005, pp 343, 349, 350. Reprinted by permission of HarperCollins Publishers Ltd © 2005 Richard Fortey

the Torridonian rocks above. It reveals a hidden landscape. When we look over the Lewisian terrain we are, literally, looking back nearly a billion years into the past ... An awesome vista of geological time suddenly opens up before us, a vision of age after age of mountain-building, of continents remaking themselves, stretching far back into the distant reaches of the Precambrian. It should provoke a sense of our own insignificance, but it also stimulates a sense of wonder that we, alone among organisms, have been privileged to see these vanished worlds, and challenged to understand the immensity of time.'

A billion years, and more, to make the rocks we wonder at and walk upon today. Meanwhile, 'Behaviourally modern humans have been around for no more than 0.0001 per cent of Earth's history – almost nothing, really – but even existing for that little while has required a nearly endless string of good fortune.' That is how Bill Bryson sums up at the end of his splendidly accessible survey *A Short History of Nearly Everything.*[22]

I would hate to give the impression that I understand cosmology, and the science of the history of the world. I am happy to lean on the skill of others for guidance, and inspiration, in such areas. But we do need to take these new discoveries on board, for reasons that we shall look at in a moment. And new they are. Bryson explains the development in understanding the age and size of the universe. In 1919, Edwin Hubble began the work that would lead to discoveries that utterly changed our view of the universe. Then, 'the number of ... galaxies that were known to us was exactly one: the Milky Way. Everything else was thought to be either part of the Milky Way itself or one of many distant, peripheral puffs

---

[22] From *A Short History of Nearly Everything* by Bill Bryson, published by Doubleday, 2003, p 573. Reprinted by permission of The Random House Group Ltd.

of gas.' 'Astronomers today believe there are perhaps 140 billion galaxies in the visible universe.'[23] Having discovered that there are indeed other galaxies, Hubble then did some brilliant observations which led him to find not only that they are moving away from us, but also that the further away they are, the faster they are going. He had discovered the expanding universe – and with it, of course, the complementary idea that one could play the film backwards and find a beginning – what we all know now, with perhaps too-easy familiarity, as the Big Bang.[24]

As for the age of the Earth, 'By the middle of the nineteenth century most learned people thought the Earth was at least a few million years old, perhaps even some tens of millions years old, but probably not more than that.'[25] Darwin had realised that he needed an enormous earthly timescale if his ideas were correct, but the means were not then available to work it out. It was not until 1953, and after seven years of painstaking work, that Clair Patterson managed to come up with an accurate figure, by ingeniously testing samples of meteorites. His figure was about four and a half *thousand* million years – long enough for the processes suggested by Darwin to have taken place.

A reliable result for the age of the universe is even more recent: Hubble made a first estimate of two billion years, and although this was later shown to be not very near the mark, it was a huge step along a road of understanding. As recently as 2003, building on the theoretical insights of Hubble and others, 'a team from NASA and the Goddard Space Flight

---

[23] Ibid., p 169 f

[24] Further useful information on the history of cosmological discovery in the 20th century can be found in Alister McGrath, *A Fine-Tuned Universe*, esp. pp 111–114. Westminster John Knox Press, 2009.

[25] Bill Bryson, *A Short History of Nearly Everything*, pp 105, 202, 573

Centre in Maryland, using a new, far-reaching type of satellite called a Wilkinson Microwave Anistropy Probe, announced with some confidence that the age of the universe is 13.7 billion years, give or take a hundred million years or so.'[26] It turns out that the expanding universe has to be old enough to have got very big indeed; and it has to be big enough in order to become really productive and interesting. John D. Barrow puts it like this: 'A universe containing living things must be an old universe. But, since the Universe is expanding, an old universe must also be a large one. The age of the Universe is inextricably linked to its size ... Even if the Universe were as big as the Milky Way galaxy, with its hundred billion star systems, it would be totally inadequate as an environment for life – because it would be little more than a month old.'[27]

It's also worth noticing, as we pass, that there seems to be a lot of slack in the system. If – and who knows? – we are the only creatures in the universe who are both conscious of self and conscious of a being to whom they owe their existence, or even, I think, if we are not, then either way there's an awful lot of universe, and however good we get at investigating it, we can assume that most of it will for ever remain out of our sight and hidden from our knowledge. Now it seems that if the universe had developed in any other way than the way it has, we would not be here to investigate it. This is the so-called anthropic principle, which says that there are 'a number of critical considerations [of how things were at some incomprehensibly short moment after the Big Bang] which, taken together, produce a fairly tight-knit series of constraints on the way the

---

[26] Ibid., p 216

[27] John D. Barrow, *The Artful Universe*, Penguin Books, 1997, p 38. First publ. in USA, Oxford University Press, 1995. By permission of Oxford University Press, Inc.

world must be in order that we are here to observe it.'[28]

It may well be, too, that the entire universe is an essential provision for our own life. We're all made of dead stars, for one thing, and who knows whether there might be some specific way in which the continued existence of our own world depends on the existence of the rest of the universe in all its unimaginable hugeness? But even if that is so, an alternative way of thinking about the creation drifts into view, provoked by the realisation of the huge amount of spare in the universe – and there really is no need for it to be seen as contradicting any scientific description of necessity. It is this strange thought: maybe God was – is? – at play. Is God allowed to have fun? Well, 'God saw that it was good,' says Genesis Chapter 1 as it summarises the work of each 'day'. He was pleased with it. In our own day-to-day lives we all know the pleasure of having done something, even something relatively trivial, as well as we know how, and simply for its own sake. Think of that writ large across the cosmos. God enjoying himself.

'Who created all these? He who brings out the starry host one by one, and calls them by name,' says Isaiah (40:26). In an age before any 'modern' scientific knowledge, he could sense the connection between the awe he felt when he saw the night sky, and the possibility of a creator. In our age, when we are privileged to have the fruits of a scientific understanding that would have been beyond the wildest imaginings even of our comparatively recent forebears, let alone of a prophet living six centuries BCE, there is no need to assume that God has been made redundant. It's equally plausible to suggest that he is still there, and that we are privy to an awe-inducing level of understanding of his methods. We would do well to bear that in

---

[28] John Polkinghorne, *The Way the World Is*, p 12

mind as we come soon to consider the very obvious and present downside of life being how it is.

Then there's evolution, which in a sense is the history of how life on this earth did indeed become productive and interesting. 'Evolution is a fact,' says John Gribbin,[29] 'just as the elliptical shape of the orbit of a planet around the Sun is a fact … The theory of natural selection, arrived at independently by Charles Darwin and Alfred Russell Wallace, in the second half of the nineteenth century, is a model which offers an explanation of why evolution happens.' We need to be careful here. There's plenty of debate at the moment around the question of just how that natural selection might take place, and we shall be using this survey of matters scientific to provide us with some very preliminary pointers in our search for a God who is not at odds with 'our facts'. So we'd better be careful to get the connection right between what science can do and what religion is for. We can see what happens if they become confused, by looking at the controversy in the United States over the teaching of 'Intelligent Design'. In 2005 a District Judge 'ruled that the Dover school board in Pennsylvania had been wrong to insist that a statement about Intelligent Design be read to pupils during biology lessons. He said such a policy represented "breathtaking inanity".'[30] A little harsh, perhaps, but the point at issue centred round the separation of church and state in the USA, and so raised the question: Is the theory of Intelligent Design science or religion? The newspaper article reporting this continued: 'Proponents of ID claim that life is inherently too complicated to have been created by accident.

---

[29] John Gribbin, *Deep Simplicity*, Allen Lane, 2004. Quotation from Penguin Books, 2005, p 175

[30] *The Independent*, 21st December 2005

During the trial, lawyers for the board argued that the school board members were merely seeking to improve science education by exposing students to alternatives to Darwin's theory based on random selection. Opponents say this is a little-disguised version of Creationism, which the Supreme Court has previously ruled should not be taught in schools.'

Angela Tilbey provided a helpful perspective on this story on Radio 4's *Thought for the Day*.[31] She makes the point so clearly that it's worth quoting in full. 'A judge from Pennsylvania has just issued a ruling on how schools should teach the origins of life. It's Darwin all the way for biology lessons – the rival theory of "intelligent design" has been banished from the classroom. In America this is one more skirmish in the long battle to keep Church and State separate.

'There are those who will argue that the ruling is narrow-minded – why shouldn't a few Christian believers have their say? Others will rejoice at what they see as yet another triumph for scientific atheism over the claims of religion. I don't see it either as a triumph or a defeat because I have never believed that creationism, which is an earlier version of "intelligent design" was either good science or good religion. Darwin did not think his theory of evolution through natural selection dealt a death blow to religious faith. In the closing pages of *The Origin of Species* he speculates on how his theory might be developed, and suggests that we might find the long progress of evolution in nature ennobling and inspiring as a reflection of just how the Creator's laws are imprinted on the material universe.

'When I hear the glorious opening chapters of Genesis being read – the story of God's creation of heaven and earth and all the creatures – what I see in my mind is like a speeded

[31] BBC Radio 4 *Thought for the Day*, by the Rev. Angela Tilbey on 22nd December 2005 © BBC 2005

up impression of the big bang, the forming of the solar system, the primaeval soup and the first molecules, primitive organisms and then all our slimy, fishy, flying, and furry ancestors tumbling into existence. The problem with "intelligent design" is that it makes me question whether it really is possible to believe simultaneously in a Creator God and in the findings of science. It forces me to choose between them, when I can't see any problem in having both. In this way well-meaning faith ends up creating doubt.

'So what of Darwin's sense that his theory was a noble and ennobling one? It's a conundrum, because he puts chance at the heart of it all. Chance is blind, but because it's blind it ensures that surprises happen; it makes this universe a place of genuine creativity. This should be a cause for wonder because it shows us something about the kind of God God is. He is not a deity who designs perfect little models and then sets them on earth to run along like clockwork toys. He's more like an artist who labours over his work, taking risks and making room for the creation to respond. More a parent than a mechanic. In such a creation it is not entirely surprising that God should be found not outside pulling the strings but, as the Christmas story tells us, right inside it, sharing the risks and chances of mortal life with the sheep and the ox and the ass, for us and for our salvation, in the cradle of Bethlehem.'

This last thought takes us well beyond where we have got to so far in our search for answers, though we shall certainly return to it. But for now, let us be clear that the faith we are looking for must 'fit the facts'. Those facts are the nature of the created order, and, in our case, the nature of whatever life events have launched us on this whole quest to find God in the dark. Failure to insist on this leads to the kind of sorry mess described above, which is a classic case of starting with a desired conclusion and then moving the facts to accommodate it. Bad science, leading to bad theology. Frankly, it's exactly this necessity to look the facts in the face, allow them to be just as they are, and then work out what kind of understanding will accommodate them, that has led to the writing of this book. In both science and theology, it's the only way we can operate if we are really prepared to seek for truth.

But we must be careful. I think we must acknowledge that there is a need for a healthy scepticism towards any explanation – scientific or theological – that claims to have everything so buttoned up as to make any alternative view laughable. The kind of atheistic imperialism promoted by Richard Dawkins falls into just that trap, it seems to me. A much more honest and helpful take on natural selection has been suggested by John Polkinghorne in his book *Exploring Reality*.[32] He says, 'While we can agree that natural selection has been an important factor in the development of life on Earth, it is by no means obvious that it is the only type of process involved ... The attempt to force classical Darwinian thinking into the role of an explanatory principle of almost universal scope has proved singularly unconvincing as it seeks to inflate an assembly of half-truths into a theory of everything.' In defence of this broader outlook he cites such evolutionary oddities as mathematics and the possibility of science; radical altruism; and aesthetic experience. These 'are gifts expressive of the nature of this world's Creator'.

So in the story of evolution, there is a balance between chance and necessity, as John Polkinghorne often points out, and there is also a God-given environment of possibility in which this balance operates. The whole undertaking is far from being a once-for-all unalterable package; it's even far, too,

---

[32] John Polkinghorne, *Exploring Reality*, Yale University Press and SPCK, 2005, pp 50, 51, 58

from being a preordained procession towards some assured conclusion. It has much more the quality of an ongoing experiment. We are poised on the cusp between chaos and predictability. Too much of the former, and nothing useful can become established; too much of the latter, and nothing new can happen.

This idea of an experiment sits rather uncomfortably with what at least in some Christian circles is often called 'God's eternal plan'. As I reflect on this rather vague concept, I realise that it was belief in such a plan, assumed to be unalterable and laid down from before time began, that made it impossible to reconcile the facts of 'our story' with belief in a God who had apparently planned everything. To put it bluntly, had God planned what happened to our daughter? Well, if his character is in any way something that we might look up to and want to imitate, then the answer is clearly 'no'. All right then, let's put it with a slightly different emphasis: *did he see it coming*? That's much more difficult to answer, not least because it requires us to think about how God may engage with what we call 'time'. This brief review of some of the scientific knowledge that we have of the world has admittedly been the work of a non-scientist, but it leads us to a similar kind of idea that I had already been dragged to by force of personal events: God, if he is involved at all in 'events', seems to have a worryingly light hand on the tiller. Now, clearly, any exposition that portrayed God as completely uninvolved in the events happening within his creation would not merit being classed as recognisably Christian at all. So we have to find a way for him to be involved, but for the future to be open, and therefore open to disaster as well as to glory. But, importantly, we need to be clear that 'open' is not the same as 'directionless'.

Eph 1:10 tells us that God's ultimate plan – the direction towards which time is moving – is 'to bring all things in heaven and on earth together under one head, even Christ'. This is such a huge thought that it's difficult to grasp. But, rather as with a piece of music, we can perhaps let the sound and the feel of it begin to sink in without having to say 'what it means'. Indeed, to do so would doubtless reduce its all-encompassing breadth, just as we can be overwhelmed by a great symphony of Beethoven or Mahler, without being able to say afterwards what it was about. So, this idea of where the arrow of time is pointing we can perhaps lodge in our hearts and minds. But there's a 'but'. The problem is that all the stuff in between – the stuff that happens now, on the way – looks very wobbly indeed.

The words of a reporter in Iraq express painfully and vividly the randomness of events.[33] 'We were en route to an interview [in Kirkuk] when a loud thump shook the air, and an acrid column of smoke billowed into the sky. A young man had detonated 80 pounds of explosives and bolts strapped to his waist. The blast, outside a mosque roughly a quarter of a mile up the road, killed 23 people and wounded more than 80. Had we arrived a minute sooner, we would certainly have been among them. There is nothing unusual about happenstance salvation south of the 36th parallel, or about happenstance death. A minute here, a minute there: the random distinction between obliteration and morning prayer.' There is a painful contrast between the experienced randomness of events and the apparent definiteness of the universe, as well as the alleged Christ-orientated direction of time, and we will have to work hard to find a God who can encompass them all.

***

---

[33] Frank Viviano writing in *National Geographic Magazine*, January 2006, p 22

Well, that's as much science as I can get my head round. But why should even that much be any help or of any relevance in what started out as a quest to find if there is a way of believing in God that fits with our experience? Well, simply this: the experience we have, which for us makes it so hard to believe, is experience that happens within the physical world. So we'd better be sure we're talking correctly about the nature of that physical world, even though the intricate detail will be lost on those of us who are not scientists. And, we must not forget, our experience is itself mediated through our own physicality. As we have seen already, that is not to say, of course, that it is 'only' physical, that to speak of physicality is to say all that can be said. There are layers, as John Polkinghorne points out. 'If interpreted experience is to be the basis of our understanding reality, then our concept of the nature of reality must be sufficiently extensive to be able to accommodate the richness of our experience ... There is an authenticity and richness in human life that demands that we take all our experience with the utmost seriousness, respecting the multi-dimensional way in which it presents itself to us.'[34]

For that reason, we will look later at how our minds may filter and interpret our experience, and how art may offer us consolation. But we must begin with the inescapable fact that whatever experience it is that poses our problem with God, it happens in the physical world, which, we are asked to believe, is the work of the loving Creator. Even if the source of our difficulty with God seems to be entirely in our heads and hearts, we must be aware that we can only experience our heads and our hearts through their very physicality.[35]

To risk summing this up a trifle naïvely, we could say that

---

[34] John Polkinghorne, *Exploring Reality*, p 5 f
[35] The philosopher Immanuel Kant was vividly, even painfully, aware of

science deals with questions like 'how?', whilst religion deals with questions like 'why?' and 'to what end?' However, they are not as separate from each other as that might suggest. If we were doing one of those Venn diagrams that we learned at school, then the circle that says 'science', and any other areas of enquiry and understanding that we might think of, and all our means of self-expression, and all our different kinds of social interaction, would be wholly within the biggest circle that says 'religion'. As far as science goes, we should be careful to note that religion cannot directly tell us about the things that belong to scientific thought; but a Christian under-standing would need to acknowledge that whatever may be scientifically true is true within the universe that God has invented. And we can go a little further and say that under-standing something about the nature of the physical world may give us a clue about how God might operate within his created order. 'Thinking about human experience in this way affords the possibility of a satisfyingly unified account of multi-layered reality. Theology can lay just claim to be the True Theory of Everything.'[36]

***

---

[35] (contd) this, and argued from it that questions of theodicy cannot be answered, since to know all that would need to be known to give an answer we would have to be God. Indeed *Dissatisfaction comes from the wish to be God. If any one claim is the message of Kant's epistemology, it is this. Traditional metaphysics could not solve the questions it posed because those questions transcend the limits of human knowledge.'* (Susan Neiman, *Evil in Modern Thought*, Princeton University Press, 2002, p 62). This led him on to the uncompromising, chilly and complicated landscape of the Categorical Imperative. I need to keep things simple: if Kant says that even asking these questions is symptomatic of a desire to *be* God, I reply rather that it is symptomatic of a desire to *know* God.

[36] John Polkinghorne, *Exploring Reality*, p 58

The attentive reader may well have seen a snag in this line of thought. The faith and Christian understanding that we are trying to regain – or, more accurately, to reinterpret in a way that will fit with our experience – appeared two thousand years ago, and out of the fertile ground of yet more millennia of Jewish history. Do we dare to add to the 'given' of the life, death and resurrection of Jesus and his religious and cultural background? (Remembering, in passing, that there was no clear divide between religion and culture in Jewish thinking, and all the better for that.) Well, add to, perhaps not; but reinterpret, most certainly. We looked earlier at a few of the ways in which Christians over the centuries have come to be aware of new implications of the Christian story. We might well have referred also to the church's shamefully slow realisation of the huge imperative in the gospel to care for the environment, as a result of which it is now limping along to try to recapture territory long occupied by New Agers, happy pagans, and many with no religious commitment but a deep desire to look after an amazing world. We are slow indeed to understand where believing in Christ might lead us. But these are not additions; they are new understandings.

So each generation has its own unique questions to ask, and its own unique problems to solve; and in that sense the way we understand and express a Christian view must change too. And of course my whole reason for writing this, and yours for reading it, is the need to come to terms – now, in our own day, it won't wait – to come to terms with our present experience that has led us to question faith and perhaps feel we must abandon belief in a God of love. But I am sure too that for each generation there is the means to hand that makes it possible to do this difficult thing, or at least to make a beginning. As we shall see later, the things we now know about how the world works may mean that, for instance, we can no longer speak of natural disasters as 'acts of God', although, bizarrely, insurance policies still keep superficially to that figure of speech. But in the same breath we can dare to say that what we now know may enable us to speak in new and exciting ways about God.

If there are new insights opening up before us, thanks mainly to the huge advances in science of recent years, does this mean that older – much older – insights are no longer useful? Has the new *logos* of scientific rationalism invalidated the old *mythos* that forms the Jewish bedrock of Christian understanding? What, for instance, are we to make of an Old Testament insight such as 'The earth is the Lord's and everything in it, the world, and all who live in it'? (Ps 24:1) Surely, for us, this can mean more than a pre-scientific 'God owns the rocks and the people and is directly responsible for everything that happens'. It can mean more, too, than the idea in the charmingly naïve harvest hymn that still gets rolled out once a year: 'All the world is God's own field, fruit unto His praise to yield.' This also may be true, but I think we can go further. If we now have the privilege of knowing something about the age of the world, and something about how life has developed, then we can, tentatively perhaps, say two things about God's involvement with the earth (and the universe), and about what it might mean to say that the earth is the Lord's. First, that in some respects he works, from our perspective, very slowly indeed – he's in it for the long haul, you might say. And second, that he seems to work from the inside, in partnership with his creation, and not from the outside by a kind of diktat. This is a world, and a universe, which is still being made. It is constantly opening up – or being opened up to? – new possibilities.

We could take a metaphor from my own profession of music: the world seems not to be so much a piece of music written in the past by a cosmic composer, and now 'performed' for his pleasure; much more, it feels as if it's still being written, and we are the notes, or the instruments. Or even the co-composers, 'made in the image of God'. Clearly the metaphor won't stretch too far, though we will return to it, but the point is that we are involved, up to our necks, in a dynamic process of creation, and no proper creative activity goes seamlessly and smoothly from start to finish. The act of creation is bumpy – or at least the results of it are.

W.H. Vanstone writes beautifully and inspiringly about this in his glorious book *Love's Endeavour, Love's Expense*.[37] Describing 'the precariousness of love's activity', he says, 'The artist is always stretching his powers beyond their known limit. If he works within his limit, proceeding by an assured programme and doing only that which he knows himself able to do, then he is no longer a creative artist ... As the artist exceeds his known powers, his work is precariously poised between success and failure, between triumph and tragedy: it may be that the work of art is marred beyond redemption, or it may be that powers hitherto unknown will prove adequate to the completion and triumph of the work ... Each decisive step is a precarious step, to be redeemed from tragedy only by the next and equally precarious step, of correction or new discovery, which must be improvised to succeed it.'

On an enormously less exalted level, I could illustrate this from my own present experience as I come to the end of this chapter. I don't mind admitting that it has been very difficult to write. Future ones will be too, I anticipate, because it's painful to look disaster in the face, and deeply uncomfortable to own up to the poverty of my faith and understanding. But this one was difficult because it has been far from my sphere of

---

[37] Taken from W.H. Vanstone, *Love's Endeavour, Love's Expense*, published and copyright 1977 by Darton, Longman & Todd, London, and used by permission of the publishers. p 47 f

professional competence. I'm supposed to know about music, not science, though this implies a distinction that would have been perplexing to many of our forebears. But I have had to wrestle with stuff that I don't deal with on a daily basis, and I have had to find a way of making the sequence of thought followable. I may or may not have succeeded, but if there is anything here that has been even slightly enlightening, then it came about through many a rewriting, and in spite of trips down many a blind alley.

In a fascinating chapter on the nature of time in *Exploring Reality*, John Polkinghorne comments on the idea, still held by many believers, that 'the fullness of times' will be an event outside time. 'I think,' he says, 'that this attitude is a mistake, for it denies the fact that human beings are intrinsically temporal in their character. Contemplation of the divine work of an evolving creation strongly suggests that God has chosen to act through unfolding process.'[38] He could doubtless have done it differently. But he seems to have chosen a 'method' in creation which is the only kind we humans can experience: one where, even if the final goal is planned, the process, or experience, of arriving at it is experimental. But on reflection I think that puts it the wrong way round. Perhaps it's not God who cuts his cloth according to how we experience things. Perhaps being 'made in his image' means this, amongst an infinity of other things: that when we experience life as having a direction, and consisting of bits that do and bits that don't come to something, we are being like God is, made as he is. Broken, imperfect, recalcitrant, to be sure. But made in his image.

It's time to sum up. This is very much the bottom rung of the ladder, but we can only go in small steps. Creation is slow,

---

[38] John Polkinghorne, *Exploring Reality,* p 123

bumpy, and a partnership. It looks much more like a process of trial and error than a seamless and guided progression from paradisal beginning, via Fall and Redemption, to glorious and eternal end. God works from the inside. Death, and only death, makes life possible. But Creation is also said to be 'good': fruitful, crammed with potential, and perhaps the result of God enjoying himself. 'Triumph or tragedy.' Let's keep those thoughts as a backdrop as we turn to look at some of the kinds of tragedy which so occupy our field of view.

FAREWELL TO PANGAEA

It [the comet] bends far over Yell'ham Plain,
And we, from Yell'ham Height,
Stand and regard its fiery train,
So soon to swim from sight.

It will return long years hence, when
As now its strange swift shine
Will fall on Yell'ham; but not then
On that sweet form of thine.

(Thomas Hardy)[39]

November 1st 1755 was to the people of the mid 18th century what Boxing Day 2004, January 20th 2010 and March 11th 2011 have become to us who live at the beginning of this new millennium. There was a violent earthquake in Lisbon, followed by what we would now call a tsunami. The river Tagus overflowed, it seems in three huge waves. Between 10,000 and 15,000 people were killed, and the city was reduced to ruins. This terrible event occurred at a time of deep questioning amongst thoughtful people in the West. The philosophical ideas of Alexander Pope had circulated widely, and had led to the idea of this being 'the best of all possible worlds'. The first section of his 'Essay on Man' (and we should note the wholly human-centred viewpoint that the title makes explicit) ends with the line 'One truth is clear, "Whatever is, is right." '

Pope believed that what appears to us as evil is just part of

---

[39] *The Complete Poems of Thomas Hardy*, ed. James Gibson, Palgrave Macmillan, 1991. As set in *A Young Man's Exhortation* by the composer Gerald Finzi.

a Great Chain of Being which could not be otherwise, and also that the proper study for humans to undertake is themselves, not God. He seems to suggest that, as we might put it now, humankind is only a bit-player, unable to see further than the footlights. Indeed perhaps there is nothing further to see. His failure or unwillingness to engage with the problem of evil is irrevocably linked to his refusal to bring God into the debate. Each can be seen as both a cause and a consequence of the other. Maybe he could get away with that when life was going well. But the Lisbon earthquake did not only extinguish lives – it extinguished any hope of thinking of this as the best of all possible worlds. Anyone with even half a brain could imagine a better world, where things like that did not happen.

Cue Voltaire, French poet and dramatist. He wrote a poem that led to a furious debate, called 'Poème sur le Désastre de Lisbonne'. Although he was by no means opposed to Pope's basic deist[40] standpoint, he wanted to express the idea that such empty optimism was untenable in a world where such disaster could happen. Rather, 'There is evil upon the earth.' This was 'anti-optimism' if not downright pessimism –more honest, perhaps, but hardly heart-warming. But this was all he had to offer, and indeed the Lisbon earthquake is also a major event in his novel *Candide*, written two or three years later. So a major tragic event led to a very serious philosophical debate – how could it not?

But the point for us is that this debate took place within a context. There were different ideas current about the nature of the world, and these were put to the test by the force of events.

---

[40] Deism: the idea that a God has set the universe and its physical nature in existence, but has no discernible involvement in human affairs beyond that initial pressing of the start-button.

In particular, where, if at all, was God, and was he responsible in any way for the world being as it is? And therefore what was the connection if any between 'natural' and 'moral' evils? Susan Neiman summarises the debate like this: 'If one believes the world is ruled by a good and powerful father figure, it's natural to expect his order to be comprehensibly just. Jettison that belief, and whatever expectations remain are unresolved residues of childish fantasy. Thus the intellectual shock waves generated by Lisbon, when noticed at all, are seen as the birth pangs of a sadder but wiser era that has learned to live on its own.'[41]

And so to the Indian Ocean tsunami on Boxing Day 2004. An event of unimaginable magnitude that led to an unimaginable loss of life: more than 200,000 people died in the immediate and horrifying catastrophe. And who knows how many more died through disease brought on by the impossible conditions in which those who survived the initial moments found themselves. It is true that to an extent it did not have to be like this. There are so many 'what ifs'. If the governments of the countries around the Indian Ocean basin had agreed to put in place a tsunami early warning system, rather than deciding not to on the grounds of its cost versus the likelihood of needing it; if one of the governments had allegedly not decided to refrain from giving out an urgent warning for fear of upsetting the tourist industry; if it were not the case that it's generally the poor who suffer more because, for instance, their houses are less substantial, or because houses in safer places are more expensive. These are all ways in which the disaster might have been made less appalling, had there been more jus-

---

[41] Susan Neiman, *Evil in Modern Thought*, Princeton University Press, 2002, pp 4, 5

tice, more wisdom and farsightedness and so on. But it would still have happened.

And, lest we should think that this was a complete one-off whose significance can somehow be reduced by virtue of its rarity, the Haiti earthquake on Jan 20th 2010 would still have happened, whatever had been the specifics of that country. Sadly, it happened to a nation already one of the poorest in the world, so that there was no chance of prior provision of housing that would have had any chance of withstanding a magnitude 7.0 earthquake. The death toll of at least 100,000 contrasts grimly with that of an earthquake in Northridge, California, in 1994. This was magnitude 6.7, significantly less than that in Haiti (because of the base-10 logarithmic nature of the Richter scale), but still an event of huge seismic force. The loss of life was in the region of 60. There were differences in population density, to be sure, but it remains the case that a catastrophe affecting a poor area will be more devastating than one affecting a rich area. We should be careful, though, not to fall into the trap of thinking that one was 'worse' than the other. There is no greater or lesser 'sum' of human misery in these events, as if we could say that because the loss of life in one was less, it could be treated as less awful. There is no sum of human agony, only the individual and corporate agony multiplied 60- or 100,000- or 200,000-fold.

By contrast, the Japan disaster of 2011 happened to one of the most 'developed' nations on earth, and the one which, by universal consent, was the best prepared for earthquakes, and even for tsunamis. Most buildings survived the earthquake, even though at 9 on the Richter scale it was one of the most powerful ever recorded. The disaster, as everyone around the world was able to see in horrifying detail, was caused not directly by the earthquake but by the tsunami, a wall of water that no one who has seen any of the huge amount of video footage of that shocking event will ever be able to forget. There were indeed substantial walls built specifically to keep a tsunami out. What had not been imagined was that the earthquake would cause the whole of that part of the country to sink by a metre, thus making the walls too low to be any use. A television reporter commented on the catastrophic failure of imagination that led planners to assume that these walls would be sufficient to keep out any tsunami that could possibly occur. But this seems harsh, and hindsight is a wonderful thing. What happened was not imagined simply because it was unimaginable until it did.

Whatever the differing after-effects, these 'natural' disasters were, as we shall see, always going to happen in a world where interesting or new things are also able to happen. Pangaea is the name given to the supposed mega-continent from which our present continents have broken into the shapes that we all recognise. From the world as we now know it, the easiest example to comprehend is the satisfying way in which the east coast of South America would fit against the west coast of Africa, and indeed the idea is confirmed by correspondences in the rock types at each edge. So the world which we imagine to be stable under our feet is in fact always on the move, and mountain ranges have been formed by the inexorable push of one tectonic plate against another. 'Plate tectonics now explains how, when oceans close and when continents collide, orogenesis [mountain-building] happens and vast mountain ranges such as the Himalayas, Andes and Alps are folded up.'[42] Without this invisible constant sliding there would be no mountains, and probably the world would be ultimately uneventful and unproductive. Maybe without this process there would be no life at all. The Indian Ocean and Japanese

---

[42] Peter Toghill, *The Geology of Britain*, Swan Hill Press, 2000, p 83

tsunamis were caused by a catastrophic undersea movement of tectonic plates. That's how the world is made. We're afloat, like it or not. So these and other events are fundamentally unpreventable. What are we to make of this? What are we to make of a world in which this can happen?

Well, frankly, it could not be otherwise. As we have discussed already, a world with unpredictability removed would not be a world in which we could be human in any sense in which we now understand humanness. But at what a cost! The question now before us is not 'Why did God make the world the way it is?' but 'Why did he make it at all if it had to be like this?' I have quoted already John Polkinghorne's honest take on this problem 'of understanding God's ways in the light of the mixture of goodness and terror which we find in the world, [which] constitutes the greatest difficulty that people have in accepting a theistic view of reality.'[43] We will look later at events of a different order, and of the sort that first set this would-be Christian on the lonely road of re-examining faith: things that indeed could have been otherwise, that did not have to turn out the way they did. Evil 'done' is very different from evil 'happened', if one can put it like that. And yet both kinds of wrong are available, possible, potential, within a world which is the only way it can be.

In *The Times* on January 1st 2005, the Chief Rabbi, Jonathan Sacks, wrote a thoughtful and compassionate article in response to the tsunami disaster of a week before. It was headed 'Why does God allow terrible things to happen to His people?' He argued: 'To wish (the natural world and universe) were otherwise is in essence to wish that we were not physical beings at all. Then we would not know pleasure, desire, achievement, freedom, virtue, creativity, vulnerability and

---

[43] John Polkinghorne, *The Way the World Is*, p 21

love. We would be angels – God's computers, programmed to sing His praise.' This seems pretty unfair to angels, incidentally, but is otherwise a fine description of what makes us human. He goes on to say, 'The religious question is, therefore, not: "Why did this happen?" but "What shall we do?"' Yes indeed, we are called to respond sacrificially at the level of love and to help and restore as best we can. But he concludes: 'The religious response is not to seek to understand, thereby to accept. We are not God ... The only adequate religious response is to say: "God, I do not know why this terrifying disaster has happened, but I do know what you want of us: to help the afflicted, comfort the bereaved ..."' He continues: 'We cannot understand God, but we can strive to imitate His love and care.' This owes more to Immanuel Kant (see footnote 35) than I think is healthy. Of course we cannot understand God in any comprehensive sense. But should we not at least try to make a start?

The Chief Rabbi's answer may be good enough within his tradition (though I have a feeling that many of the psalmists and prophets might disagree), and his desire to avoid this becoming just a theoretical enterprise is timely and wise. Our investigations must indeed lead to changes in how we act and behave. But I cannot avoid the feeling that a Christian response demands more. Why? Because Christianity has such greater pretensions, and that's the problem. If the Christian faith makes great and universal claims, then somehow it must at least permit the addressing of the big questions; the ones that ask 'Why?' and 'Can the appalling cost be justified?' and 'Did God realise what he was getting into – and what he was getting his creatures into?' and a thousand others of the kind that lurk just beyond the possibility of being formulated into anything as specific as words.

And perhaps even more than the event of 1755, the Indian

Ocean catastrophe, the Haiti earthquake, the Japan earthquake and tsunami and other disasters that seem to have followed all too frequently in these first years of the millennium have led people to ask questions about the nature of the world – but in our global village there is any number of religious and philosophical options to choose from. We could opt for the acceptance characteristic of much Eastern religion which sees the physical world as a passing and less-than-substantial phenomenon; or a God-denying view that sees this world as all there is – no more, no less; or, as I hinted earlier, we might want to take on board a post-postmodern understanding of the role played by human action in exacerbating the results of catastrophe, if not in causing it.

But the focus of this book is not to look at all possible reactions to these world-changing disasters, for that is well beyond my competence. Rather, I am asking the question: how can I believe any more in the Christian God, two of whose famed characteristics are alleged to be his love and his all-competence? And, indeed, how can I honestly commend such a God to my bewildered fellow? Consequences for belief have consequences for proclamation. Faith is like the dog on the car-sticker: not just for Christmas. The attempt by Pope, and even by Voltaire, and inherited by all the fully fledged atheistic reductionists of our day, to find a 'solution' by leaving God either out, or at least out of sight, seems like no solution at all to those of us who are struggling not to lose hold of the Christian God. I'm reminded of that painfully human remark of Jesus after 'many of his disciples turned back and no longer followed him' (Jn 6:66). It is one of those sayings that no one could have made up, and the desire to avoid loneliness and rejection is palpable. He asked, 'You do not want to leave too, do you?' to which Peter replied, 'Lord, to whom shall we go? You have the words of eternal life' (vv 67, 68). We have nowhere else to go. If this doesn't do the job, then we're lost, and even the search for meaning becomes pointless, for it is logically unsatisfactory to say that 'the meaning is that there is no meaning'. No: we're stuck with our attempt to find God-sense. Do or die.

But we established early on that our former too-easy belief isn't up to the job. In many ways, it would have been easier never to have believed – then Pope, or Voltaire, or any modern atheistic reductionist could have told the very little that there was to know. But we thought we had glimpsed something glorious – God's revelation of himself in love and power – and suddenly we're not so sure. In fact we're not sure at all any more, and that hurts. We're going to have to look at what collapsed if we're to have any hope of reconstruction. Let's put the matter starkly, so that there can be no misunderstanding. With respect: if God is in any sense going to be the solution, then he can only be that once we have allowed him also to be the problem.

So we come back to contemplating God's world, if that is what it is. Is it an exaggeration to say that it is a world that thrives on death? It's inescapable that without death there can be no life. Whether it's the death of a star that throws out into the universe the raw materials from which we and all living things are made; or whether it's the death of a creature that becomes a meal for one further up the food chain; or whether it's our own death, as we return 'dust to dust, ashes to ashes'; however we look at it, death and life are inseparable. In his entertaining book *The Stars of Heaven* Clifford A. Pickover puts it like this, in the mouth (well, mouths actually, since he has two faces!) of Bob, chief curator of a futuristic art museum, and star enthusiast: 'One to two billion stars have exploded since our Galaxy formed. I wonder if life formed on planets around some of the stars before the stars became supernovas. I wonder if the creatures knew that their deaths were essential for scattering heavy elements into the vast empty reaches of interstellar space ... Our sun is probably a third-generation star, meaning that two generations of stars had to self-destruct for humans to be born.'[44] This is the universe we have to come to terms with.

And if we select the 'zoom' option and focus more specifically on this world, then here too death is built in. Steve Olson has written an informative account of the science of population genetics, entitled *Mapping Human History*. It's also a brave book, as he makes the case that there is no basis, as we look at our genetic history, to understand humanness in terms of race. 'All people,' he says, 'are closely related through innumerable lines of descent that defeat any attempt to divide humans into races.'[45] But on the subject of the interconnectedness of life and death, he says, 'Many of the fossils that we have assumed belong to our ancestors probably represent failed evolutionary experiments, lineages of different kinds of humans that did not survive. In the end, we are the product of a relentless winnowing process, a trial by extinction.'[46] Newton famously stood 'on the shoulders of giants'. We stand on the shoulders of all the life and death that has gone before us.

But in the words 'without death there can be no life' it's impossible not to hear also an echo of what is one of the most fundamental thoughts of the Christian faith, whatever particular gloss the countless different traditions and theological

---

[44] Clifford A. Pickover, *The Stars of Heaven*, Oxford University Press, 2001. Paperback 2004, p 114. By permission of Oxford University Press, Inc.

[45] Excerpt from *Mapping Human History* by Steve Olson. Copyright © 2002 by Steve Olson. Used by permission of Houghton Mifflin Harcourt Publishing Company. All rights reserved.

[46] Ibid., p 20

stances may add to it: God gives us life, we are told, through his own death. There's a resonance here that should give us some hope as we think about the way the world is, with all its mixture of triumph and tragedy. At the end of the previous chapter we filed away the thought that our experience of a direction to time and the sense of an unfolding process may give us some clue to an aspect of the nature of the God in whose image we are made. Now we can add to that a further possibility, suggested by this linkage between life and death, and one that may come to be a hugely important staging-post on our journey: maybe, just maybe, the way God has made himself known may turn out to be more intimately linked than we ever realised to the nature of the world he has made. We'll see.

GOD OF THE BLANK CHEQUE

Tyger! Tyger! burning bright
In the forests of the night,
What immortal hand or eye
Dare frame thy fearful symmetry?

(William Blake, *Songs of Innocence and Experience*)[47]

The previous chapters have been an attempt to look at the world we know and to use it in two related ways: to see it as being able to tell us something about the ways of its Creator; and to have it as the backdrop (and the only one we have) against which we live out our experience of God. In other words, the world and the universe we live in are the context of our relationship to God – as of every other relationship and every conceivable facet of being alive. They can tell us something about God and the way he operates. This seems, I hope, pretty obvious, and a reasonable thing to do.

I have put forward our investigations into the nature of the created order in a tentative way, realising that this angle of enquiry can yield only so much. Christianity prides itself, after all, on being a religion of revelation, and is explicit that we cannot know all we need to know about God simply by exercising reason, or by observing the universe. But I have been assuming that the relatively little that such enquiry might yield would at least be 'true' as far as it went. It seems to me that this thought is in step with the attitudes of the biblical writers – from the Psalms with their celebration of many aspects of creation; through the until-recently neglected call of the prophets (and indeed the writer or compilers of Genesis) to link justice

---

[47] Publ. 1794

with care for the world; to Jesus' homely but finely observed pictures of the natural world and what they can show us of the action of God within the created order. I had thought that Dave Bookless was right to say, 'God is a great artist, and the world his canvas ... God has deliberately left clues about who he is: creation is his first chosen means of telling us about himself.'[48] I had considered this pretty uncontroversial.

Well, maybe not, and for two reasons. The first is to do with method in general, and the second with content in particular. Let's take them in sequence and deal with method first. This idea of learning about God by observing the created order leads us directly into the whole area of 'natural theology', and indeed to some extent the thoughts I am trying to express have that method as their background colour. But there are dangers. Particularly from the time of the Enlightenment, when an appeal to the 'given' of authoritative Scripture rapidly became unpersuasive, Christian thinkers began to use an appeal to the 'createdness' and order of the natural world as a way of attempting to validate the existence of a creator God. However, as Alister McGrath has shown in his recent book *A Fine-Tuned Universe*, this tended to lead not to the active God of Christianity but to the inactive (after the initial act of creation) and impersonal God of Deism. Instead, he argues, we should 'regard natural theology as the outcome of seeing nature from the standpoint of the Christian tradition'. And in fact he goes further: 'a Trinitarian natural theology brings to the observation and interpretation of nature an understanding of God that is deeply shaped by the revelational and soteriological [to do with salvation] implications of the cross. A Trinitarian engagement with nature is already marked with the sign of the cross and is thus espe-

---

[48] Dave Bookless, *Planetwise*, Inter-Varsity Press, 2008, p 21

cially attentive to the problem of suffering in nature.'[49]

Absolutely. His basic point is fundamental: we start with revealed Trinitarian thinking and then view the natural order in a particular way because of what we know, always remembering that the world is anyway understandable in the first place because it reflects and reveals the nature of God. On this point, echoing a fruitful idea from Michael Polanyi, Alister McGrath says that 'the believer's perception of nature can also be said to be fine-tuned, since the Christian tradition mandates a certain attentiveness to nature and a heightened anticipation of disclosure, which permits its noise to be heard as tune.'[50] It's exactly that that we're trying to do together. I would put it like this: we have to work with two things at once, and in order to do so we have to hold both of them lightly. On the one hand we have God's revealed activity in creation, redemption and restoration; and on the other we have all the good and ill that we see in the world as it is and as it happens. We have to be like a juggler: he doesn't grip the balls he's juggling, but touches each one only for a moment, in order to send it off on its next journey, making way for the next one to do the same, with each one both influenced by the one before, and in turn influencing the next. What we learn from observing the world – its creation and all that happens in it – must be allowed to help us understand and know the God whose world it is; and what we know of God must be allowed to help us see the world truthfully.

But that leads us to the question of just what it is that we think we are seeing. This is the second element, that of 'content' that I mentioned above, and here I find Alister McGrath's

[49] Alister McGrath, *A Fine-Tuned Universe, The Quest for God in Science and Theology*, Westminster John Knox Press, 2009, pp 58, 80
[50] Ibid., p 69

position less convincing. He correctly says that when considering the 'moral and aesthetic ambivalence of nature' we must make sure we give it a context. We must 'develop a theological framework that allows us to account for evil, while affirming the primordial goodness of nature.'[51] My problem with that is that he doesn't define 'goodness', and certainly not 'primordial goodness', leaving us, I would suggest, in some danger of not seeing the world as it really is. I believe that the idea that the universe as originally created was by its nature 'trouble-free' – to put it rather crudely – lies behind a lot of our difficulties in coming to terms with reality. As a line of explicit theological thought this is, I think, gaining a considerable level of currency. It is to be found in clear and helpfully unambiguous form, and more specifically than McGrath hints at, in *Café Theology* by Michael Lloyd.[52] This book sets out some of the background thinking that informs the ever-popular Alpha Course, which I mentioned in the first chapter, though to be fair to him and to the creators of the course, he makes it clear that his position in the section I propose looking at is his own, and not part of any 'official' Alpha theology.

Full marks to the author for devoting a considerable amount of space in the chapters entitled 'Fall' and 'Providence' to the question of theodicy which, as by now must be obvious, is the subject we have embarked upon. Full marks too for the passion with which he puts forward his ideas – he clearly is engaged with the enormity of the questions he is addressing. Not so many marks, however, for some fuzzy reasoning, including not fully following through what would be the scientific ramifications of his position, and the huge blank

---

[51] Ibid., p 80

[52] Michael Lloyd, *Café Theology*, Alpha International, 2005. Quotations from chapters 1, 2 and 3

cheque that he asks us to write in God's favour. So why am I bothering to devote most of a chapter to looking at this particular theological position, whether as found in the clear form in which Michael Lloyd articulates it, or in the much more fuzzy form that colours the background thinking of many believers who haven't quite got round to examining it in detail?

Well, the stakes could hardly be higher. The ideas put forward in *Café Theology* lead, as we shall see, to two areas of thought. The first is an appeal to a pre-Fall world in which everything in the garden (literally, perhaps!) was lovely, with the implication that the created order we now see is not the one envisaged by the creator. I don't need to labour the point that it's absolutely crucial that we come to the right conclusion about this. Depending on how we answer that question, God is either off the hook or he is not – or at least not yet. The other area of thought is a particular, and I think limited, view of the 'meaning' of the cross and the resurrection which I want to suggest is of little help to those whose starting point is woundedness or bewilderment, rather than an overwhelming sense of personal guilt. Often these ideas lie just out of sight, so it is certainly helpful to have them spelt out in some detail. Lloyd's position, which we will examine in a moment, is that the world as we know it (and, by extension, the entire universe) has gone wrong as a result of the – or a – Fall. 'We are forbidden to give normative status to the way things currently are.' All the nasty bits are no part of God's original conception for creation. So the world as we now see it can tell us nothing useful about the God who created it, since it has been changed in its very character and modus operandi from what he originally set up. If the context of our lives is a scenario so completely removed from what he intended, then in a sense there is no case to answer, and there is no need to give ourselves a headache attempting theodicy. This would be wonderful if it were true. It would give a tidy solution to all that perplexes us, and we would be free to concentrate exclusively on the story of what God has done to put things right. Of course, it's fair to say that the –or certainly a – chief element of Christian belief is something to do with 'salvation', however we may choose to define that. But I suggest that the context of that saving work is much more opaque than Lloyd is willing to accept. Reality is not something we can put into neat pigeonholes. Life is messy, and, I suggest, *was always going to be.*

As far as my thoughts here are concerned, I will be proposing that a view of the cross as exclusively and only to do with human guilt and the means of God's forgiveness is too narrow. I would not for a moment say that this view is not valid as far as it goes – but that's the point: it doesn't go far enough. In particular it doesn't go to where the wounded are. So a theory of creation that says 'the universe as we know it is so far out of kilter with God's intention that it shows us nothing of his character, or his way of working' will directly influence what we feel we can say about the cross, and will call into question whether creation can say anything that can touch the wounded. That's why this matters. This is no abstruse theological or intellectual game, to be played only by those whose inclination takes them that way. It is not a 21st-century equivalent of the mediaeval pastime of counting angels on the head of a pin. If we misunderstand the nature of the created order, we will misunderstand the nature and activity of its creator. And we are trying to hang on to the idea that its creator is also its redeemer.

As we begin to look at Michael Lloyd's particularly clear and helpful exposition of 'the Fall' and its implications, it's only fair to note that, whether consciously or not, his ideas overlap in some respects with those of no less towering a figure than that of John Milton in *Paradise Lost*. I will refer to these briefly as we go through. But I hope that it is not inexcusable hubris to suggest, in such exalted company, that there is another way of seeing the first three chapters of Genesis. So here we go. With as much fairness as I can muster, Lloyd's idea is as follows:

1) 'There is a huge gulf between how we see the world to be, and how we sense it could and should be ... The Fall is the story of how that gap opened up.' This doctrine means that 'we can make our own choices, shape our own characters, forge our own destinies'. To have made us otherwise would have removed our freedom of choice, and made him a different sort of God. The Fall shows us that God 'did *not* set up [the universe] to be red in tooth and claw. He does not engineer murders. He did not ordain Auschwitz.'

2) 'Evil, suffering and death (at least as we now experience it) have no rightful place in God's good world. They are not part of his original purposes.' We therefore have an ethical duty to try to remove them from his world. In this we are followers of the example of Jesus, who for instance raised Lazarus and was 'aggrieved at the distortion that is death'.

3) 'A world in which one species has to devour another in order to survive is not the sort of world that one would have expected a good God to create'; and it is the opposite of what we see in the Cross which 'reveals God as One who lays down His own life that others might live'.

4) Adam and Eve's rebellion against God affected their relationship with him and each other of course; but also with the natural order. 'In some way the very structures of the natural world seem to have been dislocated and disordered, and no longer work with us and for us.' Therefore 'death and disease and deformity and decay and predation ... are not the norm.

They fall short of God's purity and purpose.' 'Decay is an undoing of creation and therefore a denial of the Creator.' The Resurrection reverses this. (Here we come across the first echo of *Paradise Lost*.)[53]

5) Acknowledging that there is a variety of theological standpoints, and that what he proposes is neither part of any creed, nor, as I pointed out earlier, part of an 'official' 'Alpha' position, he then asks the question 'How did creation come to be fallen?' He repeats that Adam and Eve made their own fateful and consequence-laden decision; but points to the pre-existence of a) 'the serpent' who apparently had already set himself working 'in direct opposition to the commands of God' and of b) a creation that already needed to be 'subdued'. These pre-Fall circumstances are, he suggests, the result of an earlier fall of the angels, which skewed everything. The proper role of man coming after was a 'therapeutic vocation' by which Adam and Eve and their successors would, through their obedience, have reversed the direction of things towards a restoration of God's original blueprint for the universe. (Again, there are strong echoes of Milton in these ideas.)[54]

---

[53] 'See with what heat these dogs of Hell advance/To waste and havoc yonder world, which I/So fair and good created, and had still/Kept in that state, had not the folly of man/Let in these wasteful Furies.' John Milton, *Paradise Lost*, Book x 616-620. Penguin Classics, 2000.

[54] Milton has God creating the universe with 'Let there be light', 'Let there be firmament' and so on, only 'after Lucifer from heav'n/ ... Fell with his flaming legions through the deep', Book vii 131-134. And the calling of the newly created 'race of men innumerable' is that 'They open to themselves at length the way/Up hither, under long obedience tried,/And earth be changed to heav'n, and heav'n to earth.' They are to 'diffuse/His good to worlds and ages infinite'. Book v 156-160, 190-191.

6) We can therefore say that, for instance, evolution was not chosen by God, and the way the world works on the inside, as well as the way we see it on the outside, would have been completely different but for the Fall of angels, Man and, through them, creation. Further, in the chapter on Providence (again, full marks for introducing that much-neglected subject) he is clear that the world as God intended it would have been a world without chance. Chance is 'only to be expected in a fallen world'.

7) Next, he proposes that in this situation, as a holding operation, God *permits* suffering, but does not *commit* it. Referring to the sufferings of Job in the chapter on Providence, he says 'The author [of Job] is deliberately and carefully distancing God from any imputation of direct involvement in, or responsibility for, evil and suffering ... We need to preserve the distinction between what God permits and what He commits.' He acknowledges helpfully that we must be allowed to rail against evil, but only up to a point. When all is said and done 'the time must come when we put our hand over our mouth and find our hope in the goodness of God.'

8) Finally, Lloyd asks a question which we must take very seriously. (This is similar to no. 3, but made more specific.) He asserts, quite rightly, that 'God's purposes are Christ-shaped'. This means that we can – and must – judge events and systems in the light of his character. He then asks the question 'How do the outworkings of evolution compare with the character of Christ?' and gives the answer 'Very badly.' Evolution works by the survival of the fittest, and the weak going to the wall. 'Evolution depends upon death: Christ came to bring an end to the reign of death.'

There's lots more, and it's a good read, and certainly doesn't duck the issues, which is refreshing, brave even. But it doesn't convince this professional in the sorrows of the world.

These ideas sit uncomfortably, it has to be said, with the first chapter of the book which is a splendid exposition of creation, encouraging us to celebrate God's affirmation of physicality, and to enjoy, meditate upon, explore and look after what God has made. But if it has all gone so wrong and now bears few, or even no, marks of the character of its maker, then that celebration is a celebration of something that is not how God wants it to be. So we're in a bind, caused by a number of mistakes.

The first problem, I think, is a **category error**. He lumps together 'evil, suffering and death' and does not pause to define them, using this phrase to encompass everything we don't like, or think should be otherwise. (This is a snag similar to Alister McGrath's unwillingness to define 'primordial goodness' that I referred to earlier.) Is 'evil' only what is done contrary to God's instructions by a human being, or does it include something bad (in our view) that comes through a non-human agency? Is 'death' the dying of cells and organisms, or something to do with retaining the sense of a destiny beyond this life, whilst having lost contact with the God who might connect us to it? It seems to me that a crucial distinction between various categories of 'bad' things that happen is that with some it is appropriate to attribute some kind of blame or at least fault; whereas with others to speak of fault is meaningless. By failing to delineate a distinction between these definitions, he is obliged to fall back on a hazy appeal to some kind of imagined created order in which nothing would ever have happened – lest it be something not good. We dealt earlier, for instance, with the uncomfortable but unavoidable fact that life and death are so clearly linked that in some ways it seems that to speak of one is to speak of the other.

Next there seems to be a **timing confusion**, and some

dodgy science. Lloyd's second chapter is confidently entitled 'Fall', and he is mainstream in appealing to this concept as a way of headlining the message of Genesis Chapter 3. My NIV version gives the heading 'The Fall of Man', and indeed Milton cheerfully has this idea, along with the Fall of Lucifer, as the assumed background colour for his huge imaginative and poetic exercise. But we would do well to be aware that this word is not to be found in the Bible – and perhaps the concept is not either. To speak of 'the Fall' is already an interpretation and a point of view, but Lloyd, in company with many others, it has to be said, uses it as a given. There was allegedly an angelic Fall, long (?) before the still-avoidable human Fall. There are biblical hints of this, to be sure, but presented in such a hazy and unpackaged way that it seems dangerous and unwise to build a theology on it, especially when that theology would alter pretty much everything we believe about everything. But we'll leave that to one side, and press on.

So, we have to ask: when did this angelic Fall take place? I assume that it was after the Big Bang? Well, perhaps, in company with Milton, I'd better *not* make that assumption! If it was before it, then with things already going downhill, and even angels stepping out of line, it seems to me that to create a universe with the potential to house beings who could respond, or more likely not, to their Creator seems foolhardy in the extreme. Even if there was a sporting chance that the future God-responsive beings would play ball, the game was being played in a context where things had already gone horribly awry, and God would become some kind of celestial vivisectionist, creating sentient beings but knowing all the while that it might all go desperately wrong with them, because it already had with the angels.

So was the Fall of the angels *after* the Big Bang? If so, how long after? Had matter begun to coalesce into clumps under the force of gravity? Had the stars begun to form, with their nuclear reactions just getting going? Had any of them got to the end of their lives, exploding as supernovas and scattering their elements out into the universe, to be the building blocks of new stars and planets? You can see where this is going! If this Fall occurred at any of these points, or indeed at any other, the universe was *already* the kind of universe we find ourselves in. One where things are born, live and die, and in doing so make possible new life. To suggest that there could have been another type before it went wrong is to postulate something that we can have no way of imagining. We are being asked to write God a blank cheque. Perhaps it would have been lovely, but we'll never know.

Which leads us to a **mechanism uncertainty**. 'In some way the very structures of the natural world seem to have been dislocated and disordered, and no longer work with us and for us.' Fine: but in what way? If the angels usurped the place of God, as we are asked to suppose – and as they indeed may have done: we of all people know that there is something wrong at the heart of the universe – then what was the connection between that and the resulting crookedness of the physical aspects of creation? How did this disobedience of 'spiritual' beings come to infect so terribly the physical workings of the universe? And it's getting very complicated: we should remember that 'all things were created by and for Christ' and 'hold together' – note the present tense – 'in him' (Col 1:16, 17). It's difficult to see how this squares with a universe completely at odds with the purposes of God. Frankly, if a Fall of angels had this much effect, we're in more trouble than even we thought.

Next, and needing a rather longer investigation, there is an **imaginative failure**. Let's suppose that the angelic Fall had happened, but good old Adam and Eve had come up trumps,

held the line, and buckled down to work as creation's thera-
pists. There is a problem here already: such 'faithfulness to
their vocation' would not have been a one-off moment of triumph, surely. Their faithfulness, and that of all their descen-
dants, would have been tested with every passing second, and
the destiny of the universe would have been perpetually teetering on the edge of disaster with every half-formed thought
and moment of inattention. I would take the view that the
kinds of pickle this picture leads us into are to some extent the
result of a naïve and uninterestingly literal view of 'Adam and
Eve'. The less one takes the early Genesis account as 'history'
and the more as 'story' – or, better, as 'myth' as we saw earlier –
the more profound and fertile it becomes. But for now let's
allow them to stand there as real people, or at least as arche-
types for the first God-responsive humans. In that scenario,
their complexity, which enables them to be aware of self and of
their creator, is the result of the chance mutations of evolution,
but this was 'not (God's) original idea … it is the way things
are now, but "is not *of Him*".' [Lloyd's italics.] So their coming-
to-be has been via a process not of God's choosing, and in
some sense they are already flawed. And looking ahead, how
will their children's DNA be transmitted? Will the future be an
endless repetition of the present? If anything interesting, or
even just something different, is ever going to happen, then
there will have to be a mechanism for change. But the only
mechanism for change in a non-selfconscious organism is
chance – and chance 'is only to be expected in a fallen world'.
By implication, therefore, it could not have been operating in a
pre-Fall Eden, and will be absent from the restored Eden, and
what beckons is not paradise regained but a nightmare world
of the perpetual cloning of the whole of existence.

Or, as they step out to redeem the world as God's regents,
what will happen? Here are the trees that gave shade but

whose branches, in the old fallen world that the happy couple are putting to rights, were apt to break off and hurt the person (or animal) resting underneath. Do the branches suddenly become incapable of falling off? Would fire which had the ability to warm and to cook, but also to burn, lose one of its characteristics and become benign? Would water stay wet for swimming and drinking but become impossible to drown in? One could continue this satire ad infinitum, but the point is made, I hope. Just as William Blake's 'Jerusalem' is by no means the waffly appeal to a supposed bygone age of pastoral innocence that it is usually taken for, but a gritty piece of social protest, so the biblical account is not supposed to take us back to some imagined age of perfection. Rather, it provides a context in which we are invited to see the relationships between creator and created. The Christian hope, if we can hang onto it, is not of a return to some golden age which, I suggest, never existed, but of the coming into being of God's next thing. More of that later.

Or we could talk volcanoes, forgetting for a moment that I said in an earlier chapter that we had done enough science. For information on them I am indebted to the indefatigable Dr Iain Stewart and the first episode of his enlightening television series *Earth: the Power of the Planet*.[55] Volcanoes are a splendid example of something with huge power to destroy life, including human life, but without which there would be no life as we know it in the first place. They are the fire that we are sitting on, made visible. And without the heat within the earth there could be no life. Volcanoes were responsible for starting up the atmosphere of the early earth. Later they were responsible, by sending carbon dioxide into the atmosphere,

---

[55] BBC2, 20th November 2007

for bringing to an end the 'snowball period' when the earth froze and developing life was almost wiped out. They were able to do this because CO_2 prevents heat from escaping the earth – hence, of course, the huge danger now posed by the presence of too much of it, thanks to human unwisdom. And even now volcanoes act as a thermostat: CO_2 in the atmosphere is soaked up by the sea; plankton thrive on it, and as they die they take it with them to the bottom of the ocean; over unimaginable time they are turned into rock, trapping the CO_2; this rock is subducted and becomes molten; a volcano erupts and releases it back into the atmosphere, to start the process all over again. It is effective and beautiful and potent – but can also kill and destroy. What place for such complication in the simplistic vision of a world with all the nasty stuff removed? No – we're stuck with the dilemmas and the contradictions and the dangers.

Almost finally, and briefly after that extended exercise in imagination, there is a **failure of ethical consistency**. It simply will not do to say that God permits suffering but does not commit it. At first glance the idea seems really clever and attractive, short-circuiting all our difficulties over not wanting to hold God responsible for the bad stuff. However, at a human level this excuse, for that is what it is, would not be acceptable. If I stand by when I could have acted, I am complicit. If we didn't know that before, then we did after we had seen the pictures of the abuse of prisoners in Abu Graib. (And of course each of us with our own particular example of something terrible that was not prevented – 'Where was God when …?' – will not find it difficult to tune in to the idea of human complicity.)

But we already knew in our bones that it is culpable to fail to act against wrong when one had the knowledge and power to do so. This is only encoded in our law in cases such as the duty of a parent to care for a child, or when a carer has voluntarily taken responsibility for looking after a vulnerable individual. But we know that the meaning of 'ought' casts its net much more widely than this. And what we feel in our bones points, however hazily and imperfectly, to the fact that we are 'made in the image of God'. How can we then have a God who acts below the level of even our faulty human consciences? And the thing won't work in terms of language either. In any normal use of the word, to 'permit' implies a certain degree of approval, and also contains the idea that permission could have been withheld. Clearly we can't have God approving of suffering, but neither can we usefully picture him weighing up whether or not to permit suffering in a particular case. That god would be no more praiseworthy – or interesting – than the capricious and unpredictable gods of the Greeks and Romans, and we would be better off without him.

We simply cannot solve the problem of theodicy on the one hand by allowing God to have different (and in this case lower!) standards than ourselves; nor on the other can we use words to mean something other than what they normally mean. If we want to do that, we must find a new word. And it wouldn't be pretty.

The final point that I must draw attention to in Lloyd's analysis is the relationship between what we see in the natural world, and the character of Christ. I suggest that his conclusion, though superficially attractive, is faulty because, again, he is guilty of using **imprecise language**. He seems to be saying that evolution, or natural selection, is nasty because it doesn't act in the way that Christ acted in his dealings with people, and in his life's mission. On the one hand, life comes from death; on the other, 'Christ came to bring an end to the reign of death.' But, as we saw earlier, these are two different kinds of death. (Otherwise an unfallen world would be even more overcrowded than the one we know!) And there's more than a whiff of a **circular argument**: I don't like it, so I decide that it does not reflect the character of Christ; the character of Christ is different from it, so I decide I don't like it.

* * *

[For the sake of completeness, it's necessary here to make brief mention of the concept of Creationism, which in some ways is not so far from the Intelligent Design theory that we looked at earlier. There are of course many varieties of emphasis amongst those who adhere to this belief, but the broad idea is that the Genesis creation accounts present us with historical-scientific fact, so the creation took place in six days; that taking account of some of the dating in the Old Testament leads to the belief that the world was created in the order of 10,000 years ago; and that acceptance of evolution is incompatible with belief in a personal God, particularly with the one revealed in Jesus Christ. A survey by the Evangelical Alliance in 1998 showed that a third of Alliance church members were 'literal six-day creationists'. The other two thirds embraced evolutionary theory to a greater or lesser degree, according to the Alliance's head of theology, Justin Packer.[56] A more recent general survey by the BBC in 2006 found that more than a fifth of those questioned were convinced by the creationist argument. So we can't dismiss it as a quirky, slightly charming, oddball belief indulged in by a few well-meaning but misguided eccentrics – rather as if they were the cosmological equivalent of the faithful few who believe the earth is flat. There are many who believe in creationism of one stripe or another, and the implications are huge for how we arrive at

---

[56] Quoted on BBC online news 15th September 2008

truth, and how we use the Bible.

Having said all that I'm not sure that signing up to this set of beliefs would directly remove any of the awkward truths about the *nature* of the creation that I have been proposing so far. But it is certainly easier to move from this starting-point to saying that the creation as a whole is not at all as God intended – which lands us up not so far from Lloyd's position, though we would arrive by a rather different route. There are plenty of Christian thinkers and writers much more qualified than I to demolish the supposed wall of separation between Christian belief and evolution. My own view, for what it's worth, is that the Bible (seen as a whole and not just a few verses squinted at as though through an electron microscope) positively encourages us to find out all we can about the creation, by the use of our God-given intelligence. To decide on a 'biblical' worldview and then set it at variance with what science can tell us is a denial of one of the ways in which we are made 'in the image of God'. This book is predicated on the fact that the truth we can find from any source will never be in conflict with belief in God if he is the source of everything that can be known. However, as this and the previous chapters have shown, we're still stuck with aspects of the created order and what happens within it that don't fit comfortably with a loving and/or all-powerful God.]

So after that brief digression we must return to the particular position taken by Michael Lloyd. The implication of his thought (though as far as I can see he doesn't state it explicitly) is that Christ came to put things back to how they were allegedly 'meant to be' (my quotation marks). Sadly, I think if we take up that idea, we will never find even the glimmer of an answer to our quest: all the difficult stuff is a mistake, and will be got rid of (how? when?). Its only significance will have been that it should not have happened. No: I want to suggest a more interesting, and, I think, a more fruitful idea. Christ did not come to initiate a return to Plan A. Rather, there is a Part One and a Part Two. For now, life does indeed come from death – that is how it works in Part One, and how it was always meant to. The last action in Part One before the 'Prelude to Part Two' (where we now find ourselves) is the death of Christ. And the resurrection is the first – and only – evidence we have that in Part Two there will be a change to the way everything works: a new kind of physicality. Otherwise what are we to make of the accounts of the various appearances of Christ after his resurrection? He ate in front of his still mystified followers, yet came and went at will. He was visibly the one who had been crucified, yet was not subject to the same physical constraints as he had been before his death. All this points to the renewal of creation, and the establishment not just of a 'new heaven' but of a 'new earth' as well. This 'missing' but fundamental Christian idea is passionately and powerfully proposed in Tom Wright's book *Surprised by Hope*.[57]

It seems appropriate to think of these appearances as being the beginning of the 'Prelude to Part Two'. It is a Prelude that so far has lasted two thousand years. Speaking of the resurrection as 'an event within, as well as beyond, present history', John Polkinghorne suggests that the appearances of the risen Christ arise from 'limited intersections between these two [old and new] worlds'.[58] He insists that we have no right to devalue the old (first) creation – indeed quite the opposite. Referring to the old and new creations, he says 'the latter is the redeemed transform of the former. The pattern for this is the resurrection of Christ ... God's total creative intent is seen to be intrinsi-

---

[57] Tom Wright, *Surprised by Hope*, SPCK, 2007.

[58] John Polkinghorne, *The God of Hope and the End of the World*, Yale University Press and SPCK, 2002, p 121

cally a two-step process: first the old creation, allowed to explore and realise its potentiality at some metaphysical distance from its Creator: then the redeemed new creation which, through the cosmic Christ, is brought into a freely embraced and intimate relationship with the life of God.' This 'establishes the value of the old creation.'[59]

Hurrah for that. Mathematicians, for all the incomprehensible abstruseness of their discipline to those of us who don't understand it, refer to the concept of 'elegance' as a guide to the likelihood of a theorem being correct. In the same way, this idea of God's creation as a two-stage process has, it seems to me, what we might call theological elegance. It feels potentially fruitful. The other thing in its favour is that it's gritty. It engages with and acknowledges the difficult stuff, rather than appealing to a supposed, and entirely undefined, original plan that we are to wish had been how things turned out.

Maths is not my discipline; but music is, and can illustrate this grittiness, I think. The logical sequence, and narrative power, of a Beethoven symphony or piano sonata comes not from the inevitability of soaringly beautiful ideas, but much more from the sense of wrestling with sometimes unpromising material. His notebooks are a vivid testament to the difficulty with which he chiselled out the potential from fragmented ideas. My teacher, Gordon Green, took delight in saying that 'Beethoven was obsessed with Nothing'. Meaning that he took something that to the rest of us would have seemed of no potential value, and got inside it to such an extent that he found how it could become fruitful. This is creativity. And if we are made in the image of God, then what we understand by creativity will mirror, however dimly, the creativity of God. It seems reason-

---

[59] Ibid., p 116

able, therefore, that when we look for some theological understanding of the bad stuff, alongside pleasing elegance there will
be the grittiness of facing up to the world as it is.

***

Pause for breath. That was a long look at a particular concept
of a Fall, with its narrow implications for what we may believe
about the cross and the resurrection. If, as I think we should,
we reject much of it as wrong-headed, and the rest as un-
fruitful, are we any further on than we were at the end of the
previous chapter? Well, I rather think we are. Our goal is
beginning to look less like finding an answer to the question
'How can I understand my particular bad stuff?' and much
more like 'Where can I put it?' To which a temporary and pro-
visional answer is 'in the only world there could ever have
been – but in a world that will be transformed and redeemed.'
And as we wrestle with all this, we make a mental note that we
are 'between the times'. We are living within the Prelude to
Part Two, from which we can, and must, look both backwards
and forwards.

Three

ROGUES' GALLERY

INTRODUCTION

*Félicité becomes attached, in turn, to a rough fiancé, to her
mistress's children, to her nephew, and to an old man with a
cancerous arm. All of them are casually taken from her: they
die, or depart, or simply forget her. It is an existence in which,
not surprisingly, the consolations of religion come to make up
for the desolations of life.*

(Julian Barnes: *Flaubert's Parrot*)[60]

At the risk of too much repetition, I have stressed how
essential it is to face the facts. The facts of the way the
world works, and the facts of what has happened in our own
experience, whatever that may be; and then the difficulty of
reconciling them with faith in a loving and powerful God. One
of the most famous parables of Jesus is about the two builders
– one who built on sand, and one who built on rock (Matt
7:24–27). Jesus makes it explicit that the difference between
the two illustrates the difference between those who, having
heard his words, do or don't put them into practice. It's interesting, isn't it, that this parable is so often interpreted as asking
the question 'In whom, or in what, are you putting your trust?'
But if we read it just as it stands, its thrust actually is 'Are you
doing what I say?' And the aphorism in the previous paragraph
(Matt 7:21-23) makes a similar point and turns out to be one
of the scariest in the Bible. People may have spent their lives
invoking the name of God, even doing miracles in his name,
only to find that he never knew them. The reason? They didn't
do the will of his Father.

---

[60] From *Flaubert's Parrot* by Julian Barnes, published by Jonathan Cape.
Reprinted by permission of The Random House Group Ltd.

So we'd better be careful that we do the right thing. And what might that be, for those who have come close to losing faith and giving up on God? Well, if God is the source of truth, and we want to try to find him in the dark, we'd better start from a position of being honest about the facts. That can hardly lead us away from him.

The next section therefore is an attempt to clear away some stuff that doesn't fit the facts. We have all experienced how difficult it is to know what to say to someone who for instance has been bereaved or is going through some other deep difficulty. Do I mention it? Or is it better not to dwell on it and encourage them to look to the future? We have all doubtless made a bit of a mess of that from time to time, however hard we were trying to get it right. But the interesting thing is this: those fumbling, slightly embarrassed words that we have all said to someone who was suffering – the things we hardly know we are saying, the things we let slip just so that there isn't an awkward silence – it can be exactly those things that reveal our deepest beliefs. The instinctive response is more likely to demonstrate what we really think than a carefully thought out and elegantly framed statement, where there's time to make sure that we 'get it right'. We've all done it. And we've probably all been on the receiving end, too.

So in the 'Rogues' Gallery' we're going to start by looking at some of the things people say which reveal a world-view, and a God-view, that simply aren't fit for purpose, as former UK Home Secretary John Reid famously said of the immigration service of the Home Office. This is not in a spirit of criticism, for these words are always kindly meant, and we've all done it ourselves. But if we want to find God in the dark, then comforting half-truths will have to be ditched. I'd love to believe some of these cuddly ideas, but I think we realise by now that this search is not going to be comfortable, or answered by slick one-liners. If we're going to get anywhere, we need to venture out into the cold. If there's a path, that's where it is.

I want to avoid being critical only of others, so this section then concludes with a look at something that came into my own thoughts very soon after 'that day'. This is something I am not proud of, and find it difficult to own up to, for it is definitely not a cuddly idea; but while we are ditching stuff that 'won't do', I'd better own up to my own contribution to the Rogue's Gallery.

After disposing, as charitably as possible, of these comforts that are no comforts, we will look at some more specific theological ideas which may or may not usually be spelt out, but which lie behind a lot of easygoing Christian thinking. These too we will find are 'not fit for purpose'. This may seem a negative thing to do. But out there, on this path which is so difficult to make out, and whose goal we can only dimly guess at, we'd better travel light. We can't afford to be weighed down with stuff that doesn't work.

THE THINGS WE SAY

Out of the depths I cry to you, O Lord.

Psalm 130:1

I will not look away from Eric dead.

(Nicholas Wolterstorff: *Lament for a Son*)[61]

Just before we turn, then, to some of the things that people say when confronted with the suffering of others, it's important to acknowledge a specific difficulty associated with the particular story that my family has become involved in. It is something that I think will be shared and understood by all whose lives have been touched by child abuse. A number of people were extraordinarily loving at that time, but they were not many in number. Not because others would not have wished to be, but because the very nature of what had happened made it impossible to share it with more than the very closest friends and relatives.

An entry from my diary a few years later indicates how grief has to be endured alone:

'I am beginning to write this soon after the sad and very public death of the tiny daughter of Chancellor of the Exchequer Gordon Brown and his wife, and the day after hearing of the death in a car crash of the grown-up son of a cousin. So much grief, so many tears, such huge bewilderment. Nothing I suppose could be worse than losing the child you loved and cared for from when it was first conceived.

---

[61] Nicholas Wolterstorff, *Lament for a Son*, Wm.B. Eerdmans publishing Co., 1987, p 54

'But as I try to make sense of our own situation, I have a horrible thought. At least, I hear myself thinking, if a child dies there is a funeral, there are flowers, a memorial service, perhaps a fund for the hospital in the child's memory. At least the ghastly grieving process can begin. But with us? No public announcement, just telling selected and trusted friends and colleagues. Not that we are ashamed, but it would be no service to our daughter to put a notice in the paper.

'There's another way too in which "our story" is different, and that is the human deliberateness of it. On the one hand, a life that developed weakly, and a driver's (the other car) momentary lapse, perhaps. These I can possibly see as the necessary consequences of a physical world that has freedom built in. (Though if I were those parents, I'm sure I would think and feel differently.) Anyway, on the other, the planned execution of terrible acts over a number of years, and a teenager's deliberate act of rape. I think that this moral as opposed to physical evil is much more difficult to come to terms with. Certainly the fact that it kept happening makes God's apparent inability to act even more reprehensible. To paraphrase Oscar Wilde: To fail to save her on one occasion may be regarded as a misfortune; to fail on two or more looks like carelessness.'

It was painfully clear that amongst those with whom we were able to share this double tragedy, the help and support given was quite exactly in inverse proportion to the number of words said. A hug or even just sitting quietly with us and not giving answers was the kind of comfort we needed at that time. In that great but ultimately unresolved Old Testament exploration of the fact of evil in God's world, Job's 'three friends' started so well. They 'began to weep aloud … and … sat on the ground with him for seven days and seven nights. No-one said a word to him, because they saw how great his suffering was' (Job 2:12,13). What a pity that they then felt they had to give answers, and muddy the waters with many words. Looking back, this was a great lesson with huge implications for what and how one can believe. But for now, let's confine ourselves to a few of the phrases that kindly people let slip and in so doing revealed a picture of God and his ways that sadly won't do.

The first candidate needs to be placed within the caveat that I drew attention to earlier: I and the rest of the family and close friends were not the victims. But it hurt nonetheless. *'I know how you feel.'* Oh no, you don't. Not unless your child too has been the victim of sustained sexual abuse, and then raped just as she was beginning to rebuild her life and her sense of her own infinite worth. The details of anyone's trauma don't just define it: they act as a kind of encircling barrier, excluding those who have not experienced it. And how can even God know what this feels like? True, God as Father endured 'seeing' the death of his Son. But this feels remote and theological; only a human being can truly sympathise, in the real, strong meaning of that word. All right, so 'What a friend we have in Jesus, All our sins and griefs to bear.' But, and I speak gently and I hope respectfully here, can I really say that he, unmarried on earth, knows what it is like to see one's own child suffer in this way? So there was an oppressive loneliness attached to the all-too-real sorrow: people didn't know how we felt, try though they might, and God himself seemed a stranger to this particular grief.

So what deeper attitude is it that this admittedly caring thought reveals? I think it is this: it affirms the deep humanness of standing alongside others in their time of disaster; but sadly it makes it too easy, and fails to acknowledge the inescapable loneliness of suffering. Any person's suffering or grief or torment is theirs, and theirs alone. No one else can get inside another's aching head or broken heart. We're on our own. Ella Wheeler Wilcox put it succinctly in her poem 'Solitude':

Laugh and the world laughs with you;
Weep, and you weep alone.

If anyone is going to come alongside us in any way that would have a hope of changing things for the better, then they are going to need superhuman qualities of empathy. Otherwise the very attempt to be sympathetic only serves to emphasise the impossible gap between sufferer and comforter. Let's plant that thought – maybe it can be done, maybe the gap can be bridged; maybe there will be a Spring.

'It could have been worse.' That one really hurt. Yes, she could have been murdered, I suppose. Or left physically wounded to a much greater degree than was actually the case. (But psychological wounds are much harder to heal for being unseen. And it's harder too to tell whether they are indeed being healed.)

There are many other griefs and tragedies. Radio, television and newspapers bring them daily and unavoidably into our consciousness from around the world. Political instability is beginning to join with climate change in a lethal mixture, in the Horn of Africa and elsewhere. Or the news in June 2010 that a taxi driver in Cumbria had killed 12 and injured 11 others before killing himself. Or the horrific mass killings, mostly of teenagers on a summer camp, in Norway in July 2011. Or the horrors that slip out of the news, such as the protracted nightmare of children taken hostage and at least 380 eventually killed in a school in Beslan. That name has now joined the tragic ranks of place-names that will for ever encapsulate the worst that human beings can inflict on each other. Each of these is a trauma for each individual and family involved. Or from our local free newspaper: *News Shopper*, 27th October 2004: A family were holidaying on a beach in the Bahamas. An unmanned speedboat careered out of the sea and onto the beach. The parents managed to get two children out of the way, but their son aged 2 was hit and died. The randomness of it all, and a family whose lives will never be the same again. God have mercy on them too.

One way of differentiating between some of these sad and traumatic subjects is, as I tried early on to do in my diary, to consider that in some of them there is this element of randomness whilst in others there is an element of human purposefulness. Without in any way wishing to suggest that the suffering brought to individuals is less when it is the result of a 'natural' event or something that no human could foresee, nevertheless when someone has inflicted suffering 'on purpose' this seems to raise questions on a different and even more troubling level. It is the consequences of that kind of event that are the starting point for these thoughts on – well, on what? 'Evil'? Could this have been much worse? And even if it could have been, it still stood up, tall and jagged against the sky, as a hideous thing that should never have happened.

Here too a deeper thought lies behind the too-easy words. If 'it could have been worse', then what is being proposed is a kind of cosmic balance-sheet. Yes there's bad, but hey, there's good too, and the bad was not quite as bad as it might have been, so somehow the absence of the worst can be added as a kind of bonus to the catalogue of the already good, so good will outweigh the bad in the end, and all we have to do is wait, and especially not ask by what evidence we can be so sure that good will win. Maybe I'm being harsh, but I think that's where the logic leads us, and I don't want to waste time going there. Wherever healing is going to come from it's not from whistling in the dark.

'*God was with her.*' Well, with this one we'd better come straight to the view-from-the-pew half-theology that lies behind it. I'm sorry to say that this must be some kind of blasphemy, because it calls up the whole question of what it is to be a father. Or a Father. What do fathers do? Easy: they protect their children. As we learned each bit of our particular story, it didn't take many moments before I began to feel that I had not done my duty as a father. In cold logic, I know that this is irrational. What could I have done? Under the exact circumstances, nothing at all of course. And indeed a very helpful suggestion was made to me much later by someone with wide experience as a counsellor. She made this point: to have been able to 'think' what was happening before I knew, I would have to have had a mind as devious as that of the perpetrator, and as much turned toward the contemplation and planning of evil. This gave me some kind of comfort, that my ignorance until it was too late was a kind of ignorance about evil – better perhaps to call it a kind of innocence. Maybe I could never have known. But the point remains that had I known, I would most certainly have acted. I will come back to that in a moment, and make my own confession as promised. But the snag is, God did know, if talk of his omniscience has any meaning at all. What then would '*with her*' mean? Am I to picture God in the same room as her but not moving a muscle to intervene? So he would be worse than uncaring. Or was he an onlooker, but powerless to stop what he saw was happening, as one sometimes is in a nightmare? So he would be worse than ineffective. Paul, in his great prayer in Ephesians, kneels 'before the Father, from whom his whole family in heaven and on earth derives its name' (Eph 3:14, 15). In the light of experience, he seemed not to be a very effective or competent role-model.

To put it the other way round, we can rule out the idea that 'God was with her', simply on the grounds that this would present an impossible image of him: as knowing, and having the ability to act, but refusing to do so. Now, let's be careful. 'Refusing' only means something in the context of having the ability but not using it. 'Not having the ability', by contrast, would point in a rather different direction: to a God far removed from the all-competent, all-powerful, all-knowing (and, frankly, rather distant) God of our former belief; one of whom it might be possible to speak, amongst other things, in terms of regret, loss and unfulfilled desire. It's very, very slow, but I think we may be finding our way towards him. So maybe there's just a glimmer of usefulness to be found in what at first hearing we rightly identified as a blasphemy.

But there's another thought lurking behind this image of God being there in some way at the time, and 'knowing' what was happening. It's a thought that I touched on earlier, and it's deeply unpleasant. It's the idea that maybe (in some circumstances – but which, and why?) he may 'allow' evil to happen in order to achieve some greater or future good. Now in our case that might be for our daughter, for me, for us, or for the wider world. In his book *Lament for a Son*, from which I quoted at the beginning of this chapter, the Christian philosopher Nicholas Wolterstorff faces this one head on – and rejects it. In this wonderful, honest and touching book, he allows us to see into his heart and soul after losing his son Eric at the age of 25 in a climbing accident in Austria. 'How do I receive my suffering as blessing while repulsing the obscene thought that God jiggled the mountain to make *me* better?'[62] In our own case, this whole experience, and the spiritual search it has provoked, may lead – though on this journey I frequently doubt it – to some kind of wisdom, and perhaps to some new understanding of God and what a relationship with him might look like. But it simply will not do to say that he allowed evil, let alone willed it, in order to achieve this result. I don't think we need to go as far as theology to come to this conclusion: it's philosophically unacceptable because it would make God

---

[62] Ibid., p 97

either the architect of evil, like the essential mad baddie in a James Bond film; or the user of it, like someone finding a bit of rubbish on a skip and recycling it. Either way, he would be complicit. Whatever God's relationship is with the evil in the world, it's not that.

***

I mentioned at the beginning of this chapter the particular constraints imposed by the nature of child abuse, and it is the nature of that crime that leads me to the confession of my own which I forecast in the Introduction to this section. With apologies that this is more autobiographical than I intend the rest of this book to be, I think it's a necessity to look unflinchingly both at the awfulness of a crime, and at the unthought-out, instinctive, reaction of my own heart. It's that heart with which God must deal in my case. After looking at some things that were said by others with the best of intentions but which quite failed to hit the spot, I must sketch in my own almost unspeakable and unspoken thought. Or the definite one out of so many turbulent and conflicting thoughts, most of which, like the first state of the universe after the Big Bang, took a long time to settle into recognisable shapes and to coalesce into usable concepts. This one was different – an immediate stance towards the person who had taken away two years of a child's childhood. And, having thought that I had gained some mastery over it, I found it alive and well again one summer's day a couple of years later. It was this:

Given the opportunity, I would have tried to kill him. This, the definite wish of a lifelong pacifist! In the first case, he thoughtfully did the job for me. In the second, he was sent home from the houseparty to await our daughter's decision on whether to press charges. This, incidentally, was a further trauma that had to be undergone by someone who was already a victim. Her decision finally not to press charges was, after the event, endorsed by the trained police brought in to take charge of the case. 'We would never have got a conviction,' they said. 'And your previous experiences would have been brought up and used against you.' Once a victim, always a victim? And the two people had the same rather unusual Christian name. I would happily have killed either of both of them, and would have considered my time in prison as some kind of badge of honour.

I remember hearing a radio news report about a man who was appealing against a 14-year prison sentence for killing a paedophile who he said had molested his young daughter. The sentence was passed by a court in Denmark, a country whose famed and in many ways doubtless praiseworthy liberality extends to allowing paedophiles to form their own association and run a website. His main concern was that his daughter was alive, and safe; but as far as his own actions were concerned he was not prepared to say that under similar circumstances he would never do something like that again. That level of non-compromise I can understand, though it's not pretty. It feels like a way to assert the value of the person who has suffered, and to shout, loud enough to reach the edge of the universe, 'It was an affront. I hate it.'

I have sketched in these immediate impressions after the events not out of any unhealthy desire to go on living in the past, but, as Nicholas Wolterstorff says, 'I will not look away from Eric dead. Its demonic awfulness I will not ignore. I owe that – to him and to God.'[63] The 'not looking away' involved, for him, travelling from the USA to Austria to identify the body. But in a wider sense he refused to look away from the consequences – for the future, for the meaning of memory and

---

[63] Ibid., p 54

for faith. His short book is heartbreaking, but ultimately uplifting in its honesty. It is that dare-devil risk of looking – really looking – at what has happened, and still attempting to find faith and God-meaning that we are trying to take. No truth about God's connection to terrible things will be found unless we really face how truly terrible they are. And I rather fear that no truth will be found either unless I acknowledge my desire, which fortunately must remain unfulfilled, to execute my own summary justice. Apparently that's God's job. These acknowledgements are painful. Earlier, Wolterstorff says, 'I shall look at the world through tears. Perhaps I shall see things that dry-eyed I could not see.'[64] His book has helped me to find a little of the courage needed for that task.

---

[64] Ibid., p 26

THE DEVIL & ALL HIS WORKS

I think it's time for a brief recap. So far, we have identified ourselves as those who are trying to make God-sense of a world in which bad things happen; and we have made sure that this is a legitimate and meaningful aim. Then we tried to draw a rough and rather tentative sketch of some aspects of the nature of the universe, and of the world we live in, discovering that in some crucial respects it cannot be other than the way it is; and that there may be a useful connection between how God acts in creating, and how he acts towards his creatures. And in the previous chapter, by looking at some inadequate responses to evil, we have begun to examine in a more detailed way the events that have drawn us to this quest. In doing so, we find we have moved from thinking about physical stuff that happens because of the way the world is set up, to thinking about the stuff that happens because of the actions of people – the stuff that could have been otherwise.

However, that change from one to the other has rather crept up on us. So, as we start, we should note that the distinction between bad stuff 'happened' and bad stuff 'done' is not quite as clear-cut as we might think. We have seen that some of the consequences of the Boxing Day tsunami were exacerbated by human folly, or human greed, or human neglect, or human ignorance. And as there, so in Haiti: a year after the earthquake 800,000 people were living in camps, cholera had broken out and in spite of a huge international response in the immediate aftermath there was not a great deal of progress to see for the presence of 12,000 UN peace-keeping troops. Indeed, it may be the case that the presence of many foreigners in fact fuelled inflation to levels beyond the reach of so many poor and dispossessed.

As for the Japan disaster, it's painfully clear that the damage to the Fukushima nuclear power station made a terrible situation even worse – for those who had to leave their homes, having survived the initial tsunami, for the amazingly courageous individuals who put themselves at risk in order to try to contain the disaster, and perhaps for the future health of the region, and the seas around it, and who knows how far beyond.

Whether we choose to describe it as post-postmodern or not, it is one of the insights of early 21st-century understanding that, whilst many aspects of the physical world may be beyond our control, yet human activity may play a part – and sometimes a very significant part – in influencing the detailed and personal effects of large-scale events. The playwright and philosopher Michael Frayn puts it like this: 'As the human tribe has become ever more widely and densely settled across the face of the earth, and as we have gained ever greater control over the natural forces that affect us, so our environment has become ever more manmade – and therefore ever more the product of the decisions that we take. Once, when a river burst its banks or the crops failed, we wondered helplessly at the inscrutable decisions of God. Now the media investigate why the constituted human authority took a decision to save money on flood barriers or irrigation canals. Or why it failed to take a decision at all – because the failure of foresight and imagination, too, is a human responsibility. Human choice (where determined or not) accounts for more and more links in the great causal chain that we perceive.'[65]

The current debate and concern over global warming is just such an area. Let's pray that we are not too late, but over the

---

last twenty or thirty years the human family has discovered that the climate on whose reliability we depend, is very much subject to the way we humans treat the world. On the one hand, climate functions autonomously, whether there are any humans to appreciate it or not. On the other, the way we live and squander the earth's resources results in our receiving from the climate a very different result than would be the case if we had acted less selfishly. In fact, that should be 'if we had acted according to the view of creation that the Bible presents'. What a tragedy that Christians couldn't see it until it was possibly too late.

Another keenly felt example of the mixing of what we cannot control and what we can, or should have, controlled, is the aftermath of Hurricane Katrina in New Orleans in August 2005. We cannot know to what extent the severity of this event was due to climate change. But, without a doubt, the results of it were made worse than they might have been by government inaction, and an apparent failure to see that the poor needed – if anything – more care, rather than less, if they were to survive and be restored.

A report by Oxfam in 2008 showed that poor decisions and bad management cause more deaths in the wake of natural catastrophes. Oxfam's south Asia regional director said, 'The Kashmir earthquake [of 2005] killed 75,000 people. That's more than 12 times as many people as died in Japan's Great Hanshin [or Kobe, 1995] earthquake, which was of similar strength. Why? Poverty, exclusion, inequality and unsuitable policies raise risks for poor people, women and minorities especially.'[66] And it works the other way round, too, in terms of what the world community ought to do better. Another Oxfam

---

[66] Quoted in *Metro* newspaper April 10th 2008

report[67] made the telling point that 'climate change was first seen as a scientific problem, then an economic one. Now it is becoming a matter of international justice.'

So, as we continue our look at quasi-Christian ideas that 'don't fit the facts' we need to remember that there is at best a very hazy dividing line between ourselves as those who experience disaster or share in the disaster of others, and any agencies at whose door we might be inclined to lay the blame. It will come as no surprise then that the next culprit we must turn our attention to is the devil – or 'the accuser', as the Bible usage might be better translated.

The devil and death

Perchance he for whom this bell tolls may be so ill as that he knows not it tolls for him ... Any man's death diminishes me, because I am involved in mankind; and therefore never send to know for whom the bell tolls; it tolls for thee.

(John Donne)[68]

The standard culprit in Christian understanding of evil is the devil. This is so much part of our fundamental understanding that to state it baldly as I have just done sounds like an embarrassing statement of the obvious. But let's be brave and look carefully at what's being said. In his Introduction to C.S.Lewis's *A Grief Observed*,[69] his stepson Douglas H. Gresham writes: 'He

---

[67] Reported on BBC online news 9th Sept 2008. Report author: Kate Raworth

[67] John Donne, *Meditation xvii*

[69] *A Grief Observed* by C.S. Lewis copyright © C.S. Lewis Pte. Ltd., 1961. Extracts reprinted by permission.

[Lewis] had written also about the great poets and their songs of love, but somehow neither his learning nor his experiences had ever prepared him for the combination of both the great love and the great loss which is its counterpoint; the soaring joy which is the finding and winning of the mate whom God has prepared for us; and the crushing blow, the loss, which is Satan's corruption of that great gift of loving and being loved.'

Well, is it? This self-proclaimed professional vis-à-vis the sorrows of the world begs to differ. We cannot blame the devil for the fact of physical death. We've seen already that death is built into the nature of the physical universe. So in this creation, whose character we have been trying to discern, to find love and commitment means almost certainly for one partner to experience loss. Total loss – of the one with whom he or she had become one flesh: so much more than bodily union, overwhelming though that can be. We are talking about the process of becoming someone else, through the all-pervasive influence of shared lives. And then half of that new, growing creature is removed – excised without anaesthetic, leaving the scar of the scalpel for all to see, and leaving the bereaved dismembered. I'm afraid it won't do to say that God meant it otherwise, and the devil spoiled it. He has spoiled much, but not some imagined world in which death was absent.

Nor will it do to play down death. There is a poem which crops up regularly in funeral services, and which I have seen amongst the 'helpful thoughts' offered by undertakers and by the kind people who minister to those whose relatives have died in hospital. It is by Henry Scott Holland (1847–1918). He was a Canon of St Paul's Cathedral, and should have known better. What he wrote is well known, but it is a lie.

Death is nothing at all.
I have only slipped away into the next room.

I am I and you are you,
whatever we were to each other, that we still are.
Call me by my old familiar name,
Speak to me in the easy way which you always used.
Put no difference in your tone,
wear no forced air of solemnity and sorrow,
laugh as we always laughed
at the little jokes we enjoyed together.
Pray smile, think of me, pray for me.
Let my name be ever the household word
that it always was.
Let it be spoken without effort,
without the trace of a shadow in it.
Life means all that it ever meant,
it is the same as it ever was.
There is unbroken continuity,
why should I be out of mind
because I am out of sight?
I am waiting for you
somewhere very near
just around the corner.
All is well.[70]

Actually, it's rotten poetry as well, but that's the least of our
worries. Let's be kind: Canon Holland presumably thought he
was offering words of comfort that would ease the pain of loss.
But this is truly fool's gold. Had he never come across Romeo
and Juliet, or heard the Liebestod from Wagner's *Tristan and
Isolde*? I am writing this, as it happens, shortly after the death

---

[70] The King of Terrors: a sermon delivered in St Paul's Cathedral on
Whitsunday 1910, while the body of King Edward VII was lying in state
at Westminster; publ. in *Facts of the Faith*, 1919

of my father-in-law. He was 85, had unshakeable faith in God, and had made it clear that he was ready to die – to 'go home' as he liked to put it. But it's absolutely clear that he has not slipped away into the next room. He is not just around the corner. Continuity has been broken. There's nothing to be gained by pretending: he's gone, and it hurts, and his wife of 62 years and family and friends will live the rest of their lives without him.

Wordsworth has something more honest to say (and in better poetry).

> *Surprised by joy — impatient as the Wind*
> *I turned to share the transport – Oh! with whom*
> *But Thee, deep buried in the silent tomb,*
> *That spot which no vicissitude can find?*
> *Love, faithful love, recalled thee to my mind –*
> *But how could I forget thee? Through what power,*
> *Even for the least division of an hour,*
> *Have I been so beguiled as to be blind*
> *To my most grievous loss? – That thought's return*
> *Was the worst pang that sorrow ever bore,*
> *Save one, one only, when I stood forlorn,*
> *Knowing my heart's best treasure was no more;*
> *That neither present time, nor years unborn*
> *Could to my sight that heavenly face restore.*[71]

This is bleak, perhaps. But we might as well look the thing in the face. That's what happens in a world where everything dies and life feeds on the remains of death. Let's not have any compunction about this: whatever else may be the devil's fault, it's not this. It's the way the world is. God's world has death built in, and it's no use blaming the devil. John D. Barrow, writing

---

[71] William Wordsworth, *Surprised by Joy*.

about what he calls the 'impact' of evolution, makes an interesting point by doing a thought-experiment about mortals and immortals. 'Death and periodic extinctions play a vital role in promoting the diversity of life … The sudden extinction of species allows the evolutionary process to accelerate. In this respect, immortals would evolve more slowly than mortals. Immortality also does strange things to urgency.'[72] He goes on to quote from a brilliantly inventive story by Alan Lightman about a world in which everyone lives for ever. 'Its society splits into two quite different groups. There are procrastinators who lack all urgency … By contrast, there were others who reacted to the unlimited time by becoming manically active because they saw the potential to do everything. But they did not bargain for the dead hand that held back all progress, stopped the completion of any large project, and paralysed society. It was the voice of experience. When every craftsman's father, and his father, and all his ancestors before him, are still alive, then experience ceases to be solely of benefit. There is no end to the hierarchy of consultation, to the wealth of experience, and to the diversity of alternatives. The land of the immortals might well be strewn with unfinished projects, riven by drones and workers with diametrically opposed philosophies of life. With time to spare, time might not have spared them.'

So what are we to make of all the Bible references to the intimate connection between sin (the devil's province) and death? What appears to be an explicit connection between the two is made by Paul in Rom 5:12. 'Sin entered the world through one man [Adam], and death through sin, and in this way death came to all men, because all sinned.' It's difficult –

---

[72] John D. Barrow, *The Artful Universe*, p 41 (by permission of Oxford University Press, Inc). Quoted material from A. Lightman, *Einstein's Dreams*, Bloomsbury, London, 1993.

perhaps impossible – at this distance to know what kind of death Paul had in mind. However, with present knowledge we can be sure that the fact of physical death is not caused by the alienation of humans from God. The one did not cause the other, for the rather straightforward reason that there was plenty of death before there were humans able to respond to, and to turn away from, God. I remember being troubled as a child by the apparent absurdity of a one-to-one connection between death and what we may or may not want to refer to as the Fall. If there had been no Fall, my reasoning went, people would not have died, and the world would be very full, and mostly with very old people! So the Fall became the merciful agent of a kind of divine cull, preventing over-population. Which made it a good thing. Which it clearly wasn't.

John Polkinghorne has a useful take on this conundrum. 'We can today interpret those words in Romans,' he says, 'in the sense of referring not to fleshly death but to what may be called "mortality", spiritual sadness at the transience of human life.'[73] And, I would want to add, sadness at the loss of hope. I am happy to blame the devil for inducing in humanity an alienation from God, which makes death the final architect of our despair. But it is unreasonable to blame him for the fact of physical death. It is God who must answer for this fundamental fact of his creation. And it is to try to find some basis for the restoration of hope that this is being written.

---

[73] John Polkinghorne, *Exploring Reality*, p 139

The devil and evil

The man said, 'The woman you put here with me – she gave me some fruit from the tree, and I ate it.' The woman said, 'The serpent deceived me, and I ate.'

Gen 3:12, 13

So if we can't blame the devil for death, can we blame him for how we or others behave? At least in matters involving human action and will, surely we can blame the devil for being active in the world, and appeal to the overarching Christian idea that God in Christ has won the victory over the devil, though there is still a lot of 'mopping up' to be done. This may all be true, but I think there is a danger of sidestepping the issue. When Hansie Cronje, the Christian South African cricketer, was found to have been involved in match-fixing, he said, 'The devil got into me,' or words to that effect. Maybe that is a fair description on one level of what happened, but Cronje was not thereby excused. He could not avoid his own responsibility. He did it, and meant to. And of course we all can and must put our own names and details into the blanks of that sentence. I find it dishonest to blame an outside party for my own failings, and for other people's. It feels like a cowardly sort of cheating to appeal to a 'diabolus ex machina' to explain all the bad stuff done by me or others.

A very helpful 'definition' of the identity and activity of 'the satan' as he prefers to call it is given by N.T. Wright. 'The biblical picture of the satan is ... of a non-human and non-divine quasi-personal force which seems bent on attacking and destroying creation in general and humankind in particular, and above all on thwarting God's project of remaking the world and human beings in and through Jesus Christ and the

Holy Sprit.'[74] This I think gives proper weight to his (its?) presence in the background of the landscape of our discussion. But it gives us no reason for thinking that by accusing the accuser we can wave goodbye to human responsibility.

I referred in an earlier chapter to Walter Wink's monumental study *Engaging the Powers*. His overarching idea is that there are powers outside (I hesitate to say 'above') our human level which are fallen, but redeemable. For instance, he would say that a large organisation for which we might work has a 'spiritual' identity which may be thought of as the combination of the attitudes and actions of all its members, but which then (to paraphrase with an idea that I think he doesn't actually use himself) develops a life of its own. This may then turn out to be skewed away from the gracious purposes of God. Explaining how this might relate to the concept of a devil, or satan, he says, 'We are speaking now of a deeper evil – a layer of sludge beneath the murky waters that can be characterized only as a hellish hatred of the light, of truth, of kindness and compassion, a brute lust for annihilation. It is the sedimentation of thousands of years of human choices for evil (not *wrong* choices merely, but actual choices *for* evil) that has precipitated satan as the spirituality of evil. Call it what you will, it is real.'[75]

Remember that earlier we said that our task was beginning to look less like a search for how to understand the bad stuff, and more like a search for where to put it. It seems to me that even if we could come to some deep understanding and awareness of the existence and activity of a satan, this would not help us very much towards finding a place to put the bad stuff. As I tried to clear the ground in earlier chapters, I had been

[74] N.T. Wright, *Evil and the Justice of God*, p 70
[75] Walter Wink, *Engaging the Powers*, p 69

thinking that when we came, as we now have, to consider evil done by humans, distinct, as far as we can make it, from bad stuff that comes wrapped up with the nature of the world, then the going – philosophical and theological – would get even tougher. But maybe I was wrong. The problem is not really the 'why' of human wrongdoing – call it sin if you like. It's clear to all but the most ardent scientific atheist that there is within us all a capacity for evil, and perhaps a deep-down inability to say no to it, or at least to live up to our own standards. We could define sin as what results from a profound dislocation from God. As I mentioned in an earlier chapter, this is the default starting-place for most Christian exposition of the fundamentals of the faith. But it is not what we, the community of the bewildered, need as of first importance.

If then the question of the 'why' of human wrongdoing is not going to help us, the problem we do need to address is to be found in an awkward and uncomfortable place. It does indeed ask 'Why?', but not 'Why is there sin?' It's a triple whammy: the 'why' of the nature of God's creation, with its inbuilt potential for glory and disaster; the 'why' of God's apparent inability to prevent specific instances of human evil, even if we permit him to be unable to prevent the evil that cannot be put down to deliberate human sin; and, following from both of those, the 'why' of what appears to be his method of dealing with it. In other words: the apparent limits of his power; and the slow and seemingly unspecific results of whatever it was he intended by the incarnation, death and resurrection of Jesus.

So we have lodged our quest, our problem that needs to be solved, firmly in a particular place – the character and actions of God. And the place we shall begin to find some pointers to the way God acts is in the storehouse of his creativity. There we may be able to discern enough of the way he goes about things as a creative being, to be able to look for some parallels with how he may have gone about the business of dealing with evil. Before we put that under the spotlight, though, there are two final theological horrors that we must identify and then throw out with all the energy we can muster.

Bring on the Good Times

No 'Back to the Future'

God said to Moses, "I AM WHO I AM."

Exod. 3:14

Love's not Time's fool, though rosy lips and cheeks
Within his bending sickle's compass come:
Love alters not with his brief hours and weeks,
But bears it out even to the edge of doom.

(Shakespeare)[76]

The film *Back to the Future*, and countless episodes of *Star Trek* and similar kinds of science fiction, are predicated on a fascinating conundrum. If, and it's a big 'if', we could go back in time, could we alter the course of history? This thought experiment throws up all sorts of apparent impossibilities. If, knowing what I know, I could rush up those stairs in Dallas in 1963, wrestle Lee Harvey Oswald to the floor and 'save' President Kennedy, what would then become of the career of Lyndon B. Johnson, who was immediately elevated to the Presidency when Kennedy died? And there is potential for lots of science fiction fun to be had with the idea of a child returning to a time before his own birth and meddling in the lives of his parents-to-be. Somewhere deep in our minds we know that, whatever convoluted exit strategies a fiction writer may employ to square this circle, in the real world these impossibilities tell us that the past cannot be tampered with. It is what it is. The arrow of time.

---

[76] from Sonnet 116

But in trying to come to Christian terms with those aspects of the past that we fervently wish had been otherwise, there is a great temptation to employ a rather similar process of thought. We try to convince ourselves that because – perhaps at some distance in time from the event – we can begin to see dimly something 'good' that may have grown out of the original 'bad', then the bad was perhaps not so bad after all. But the 'badness' is not simply a matter of perception, as if it were something that could be altered by squinting at it in a different way, or from a greater distance. Or as if just because some perhaps wonderfully beautiful flower is now growing out of the soil of the original bad thing, the bad thing no longer counts.

Now, we need to unpick this dangerously attractive idea with care and a clear head. It's obvious that good things can come out of bad – and we can even say that without the bad, some good might not have come to pass. There are many instances of those who have channelled grief towards the service of others. They may set up funds in memory of a loved one, or work to make it less likely that what happened to them will happen to others. For instance, relatives of victims of road accidents have campaigned for better road safety awareness. Many of those at the forefront of the peace movement in Northern Ireland had themselves been closely and personally touched by the 'troubles'. More recently, in September 2006, one of the presenters of the television programme *Top Gear*, Richard Hammond, crashed a jet-powered car at almost 300 mph in a stunt being filmed for the programme. He was rescued, and his life probably saved, by paramedics from the air ambulance service. A website was set up as a result of the huge publicity the event engendered, and in just a few days enough money had been given by the public to buy a new helicopter. Good from bad, indeed.

It's worth also noticing in passing that such a public

response to a very public and highly publicised event is possible only in the global village which we now inhabit, thanks to the instantaneous dissemination of news through radio, television and the internet. This was vividly illustrated in the outpouring of practical concern and giving following the Indian Ocean tsunami in 2004, the Pakistan earthquake in 2005, the Haiti earthquake in 2010, and the Japan tsunami in 2011, to name only the most prominent recent examples. But this coming together of the worldwide community, where what happens on the other side of the world is in our living rooms within minutes, only renders still more vivid our awareness of the fundamental problem that we are trying to think about: we, more than any generation before us, know, and cannot avoid knowing, that the world is dark and dangerous and that few people get through life without experiencing some kind of disaster or trauma.

Walter Wink expresses powerfully this vivid awareness of the world's sufferings in his book from which I have quoted already. 'The groaning of the Spirit within us is related to the groaning of the created order, subjected, as it is, to futility (Rom 8:20). We are inundated by the cries of an entire creation: the millions now starving to death each year, the tortured, the victims of sexual abuse or battering, the ill. But that is not all: we also bear inexpressible sorrow for all the species that have become extinct and those on the verge of extinction, the plants and trees and fish dying of pollution, the living beings dislocated or killed by forest fires, hurricanes, volcanic eruptions, and the like. We are so interconnected with all life that we cannot help being touched by the pain of all that suffers. The more highly developed our consciousness becomes, the more terribly the knowledge and anguish of that suffering weighs on us, till we risk being crushed by it. It seems to me that more and more people who never experienced depression before are aware of being episodically depressed today. I do not believe their depressions are neurotic, but a sign of potential health: their heightened capacity to take in the suffering of the planet. There is something impersonal and objective about these depressions that bespeaks a high degree of moral development. The world has shrunk … We are literally inundated with news of suffering from all round the globe, and it cannot but affect us. How much more, then, those who have deliberately opened their hearts to humanity as one family in God? … But we must not try to bear the sufferings of the creation ourselves. We are to articulate these agonizing longings and let them pass through us to God. Only the heart at the centre of the universe can endure such a weight of suffering.'[77]

More, much more, of that later. But for now, as we have seen, this world-awareness can lead to acts of deep personal intention – to heal wounds, to restore loss, to learn from tragedy. But there's a 'but'. Notwithstanding the good that can be born out of the bad, and indeed the good that is simply born out of goodness, and which we can see around us at any moment, we cannot say that the bad is thereby deemed not to have been so bad after all. This is a category mistake in regard to the direction of time. A beneficial outcome cannot be sent in reverse against the flow of time, there to reinvent the original happening. So we are wrong if in our imagination we try to review – re-view – the event in the light of subsequent developments. It's easy to do this, and many comments by genuinely concerned and well-meaning friends may well encourage us to do so. 'It's all turned out for the best' – I think not. 'The best' is already ruled out because 'the worst' happened. Or: 'Think of the good that's come out of it' – well, possibly, but 'it' still is, and forever will be, something bad. The

---

[77] Ibid., p 304

trauma that was will forever remain that, a trauma that had to be lived through and that has to be lived with into the future. Time may heal, but it doesn't rewrite.

We can take this thought further. The person that each of us is, is the product of the sum of our past. The occasional tragic cases of patients who lose all but the most recent few seconds of memory illustrate how we are what we were. With no ability to anchor the self in history, most of what we think of as 'the self' appears to be wiped out. An eternal present forbids the sufferer to know himself and to grow in any sense other than a slow growing old. Our self-consciousness, or self-awareness, is the chief thing by which we know that we are 'different' from the animals. And this crucial thing that makes us human is intimately linked to our ability, when we are healthy, to view ourselves as standing at the leading point of the line of our history. There's a lovely line in Alan Bennett's play *The History Boys* when an unruly class of adolescents is asked by the teacher, 'What is history?' Quick as a flash, one of them replies, 'It's just one thing after another.' That is what, and who, we are. Out of the mouths of adolescents and playwrights.

A news article in *The Guardian* (3rd February 2006) explained that at some time in the (near?) future, scientists might succeed in creating a pill to deal with post-traumatic stress. The implication appeared to be that it would work not by enabling the individual to deal in the present with the distressing effects of a past trauma, but by somehow wiping out the memory of the trauma itself. This has disturbing echoes of Orwell's nightmare vision in *Nineteen Eighty-Four*, which is reason enough to fear it, but taken just as it is, it would surely somehow only diminish the individual. Our task in this investigation is much more difficult and disturbing. It is to acknowledge that the bad goes on being bad, and cannot be wished or pretended out of existence; and then to try to find where on earth – or in heaven – we can make contact with a God who is loving enough to care about it, but apparently was unable to prevent it. To refer briefly to our own story, we now proudly see a daughter who is a member of one of the emergency services, and so spends her life ministering to people experiencing trauma. The connection with past history is not difficult to spot. But that connection is not able to make any comment on the earlier events. If God is to find us, he will have to find us as the people we are, with this – whatever it is – on board, written into our history, and part of who we are today. We can neither reinvent the past, changing our view of it because of how things may have turned out, nor live our lives without it.

Somewhere over the rainbow

What would the world be, once bereft
Of wet and of wilderness? Let them be left,
O let them be left, wildness and wet;
Long live the weeds and the wilderness yet.

(Gerard Manley Hopkins: *Inversnaid*)[78]

The only partly casual mention of heaven a moment ago brings us to the last of our 'easy answers' that simply won't do. A superficially similar suggestion to the ideas we have just been looking at is often put forward in Christian thinking as a way of coming to terms with the bad stuff. Put only slightly more crudely than one often hears it articulated, it is this: this world is just a preparation for the next, and when we get there all the memories of grief and anguish will be blotted out by the sound

---

[78] Gerard Manley Hopkins, *Poems and Prose*, Penguin Classics, first publ. 1953, p 50

of general rejoicing, and all that pain will have no more reality than a dream fading as we wake.

C.S. Lewis toys with this idea in *The Last Battle*, the final book in the 'Narnia' series. Some of the children from the earlier books are introduced quite late into the narrative. Eustace explains: 'There we were in the train. And we were just getting to the station where the others were to meet us, and I was looking out of the window to see if I could see them when suddenly there came a most frightful jerk and a noise: and there we were in Narnia and there was your Majesty tied to the tree.'[79] At the end of the book, C.S. Lewis writes this: 'Lucy said, "We're so afraid of being sent away, Aslan. And you have sent us back into our own world so often." "No fear of that," said Aslan. "Have you not guessed?" Their hearts leaped and a wild hope rose within them. "There *was* a real railway accident," said Aslan softly. "Your father and mother and all of you are – as you used to call it in the Shadowlands – dead. The term is over: the holidays have begun. The dream is ended; this is the morning."'[80]

It's beautifully and poetically put, and well expresses the idea that although we can know little about it for sure, we harbour a deep assumption that 'heaven' will be 'better'. 'Solid joys and lasting treasures none but Zion's children know', as the old hymn puts it. But somewhere behind all this is the thought that what we found so appalling here, when we went through it, will turn out not to have been so appalling, or so substantial, and, crucially, will not need to be referred to again. In which case I would suggest that the person that each of us is, by virtue of his or her 'history', would be incomplete.

---

[79] C.S. Lewis, *The Last Battle*, copyright © C.S. Lewis Pte. Ltd., 1956, p 50. Extracts reprinted by permission.
[80] Ibid., p 165

In any case, it feels unsatisfactory to say that this life is only a rehearsal for the real performance which is to come. Would God have invested so much time and creativity in something that was only 'Shadowlands'? If this world, with its glories and disasters, feels only too substantial, I would suggest that that is because it is indeed substantial and real – and meant. As we saw earlier, the universe is old, and the world is made of hard rocks, and we are made of stars. God seems to do physicality. The shamefully overlooked concept of 'the resurrection of the body' is, or ought to be, a fundamental element in a Christian understanding of what happens after death, and of how we could think about 'taking our history with us'. Rather than saying that 'now' will turn out not to have been much to speak of, we must do the more difficult thing, which is to envisage a future life into which we take our all-too-real history.

At the start of this book we noticed briefly the promise in Revelation 7:17 that 'God will wipe away every tear from their eyes'. There will be tears there, or at the very least the memory of tears. There, doubtless, we may be healed, de-traumatised, made new – but not by means of a lobotomy of memory. John Polkinghorne is alert to the danger of invoking heaven as a way of softening the blow of the present. 'The Christian has to exercise great discretion in appealing to the life of the world to come. A facile invocation of future good as the means of explaining away present ills can be insensitive and unconvincing,' though he adds the important caveat that at the same time we must 'affirm the eschatological hope of the ultimate absolute triumph of good over evil.'[81]

I mentioned in an earlier chapter C.S. Lewis's *A Grief Observed*. It was written in the white heat of the loss of his

---

[81] John Polkinghorne, *Exploring Reality*, p 145

beloved wife Joy, whom he had found only a few years earlier.
He is clear that whatever we may mean by heaven, in one sense
it's not going to be much help. 'Talk to me about the truth of
religion,' he says, 'and I'll listen gladly. Talk to me about the
duty of religion and I'll listen submissively. But don't come
talking to me about the consolations of religion or I shall sus-
pect you don't understand. Unless, of course, you can literally
believe all that stuff about family reunions 'on the further
shore,' pictured in entirely earthly terms. But that is all unscrip-
tural, all out of bad hymns and lithographs. There's not a word
of it in the Bible. And it rings false. We *know* it couldn't be like
that. Reality never repeats. The exact same thing is never taken
away and given back. How well the spiritualists bait their hook!
"Things on this side are not so different after all." There are
cigars in heaven. For that is what we should like. The happy
past restored.'[82] How right he is to rail against this.

I blame Plato. (And the Victorians, whom we'll deal with in
a moment.) Christian thought was early on seduced by Greek
ideas of perfection. The Platonic concept of 'forms' was that
there was a perfect version of everything that we are able to
think of. This could be apprehended by thinking backwards,
as it were, from the thing we know, whether an object or an
idea, to the 'perfect' version of it. The thing we know is only an
imperfect reproduction of the perfect version that exists in
another realm. Crucial for our purposes here is the corollary
that being perfect, it could not change. Because 'well-educated
Jews [were] well aware of the parallels between Jewish and
Hellenistic ideas',[83] it was easy for these modes of thought to
pass into early Christian thinking. So it seemed obvious for
Christians to think that both God and his heaven must be

---

[82] C.S. Lewis, *A Grief Observed*, p 25
[83] John Polkinghorne, *Exploring Reality*, p 181

static, because by definition they are perfect. And from there it's the work of a mere moment to conclude that all that nasty stuff that happened in real time will be forgotten and abolished, because time will be wiped out, so all we need to do is wait for the mercy of that forgetfulness.[84]

This idea has slipped deep, but unnoticed, into standard Christian thought, and needs to be radically excised. Gregory Boyd, in the book I referred to earlier, puts it like this: 'A fundamental aspect of classical theological thinking, again revealing the influence of Plato, was that God experiences no "before" or "after." He experiences all of time in a single, changeless, eternal moment. We have to ask, however, Where is this notion taught in the Bible? Doesn't every page of the Bible paint a portrait of a God who experiences things, thinks things, and responds to things *sequentially*? Every verb applied to God in the Bible testifies to this. The God of the Bible is alive, dynamic, personal, changing, free, and relational. How different this is from the static, unchanging, wholly necessary God of Plato and much of the church's classical theology.'[85]

These attributes of God will serve us well in a moment, when, as advertised earlier, we finally come to investigate the links between the modus operandi of God in creation and in salvation. But for now let us be encouraged to abandon any idea that the life beyond death will be static, and so unrelated to this life that there will be no connection between present sorrows and future bliss. N.T. Wright splendidly satirises the 'ontological dualism' which 'says that the world of space, time

---

[84] It is possible that St Paul is skirting round this idea in his paean to love in I Cor 13:10: 'when perfection comes, the imperfect disappears.' But here he is making a contrast between things that will no longer be needed in the future existence, such as prophecy, and love which 'never fails'.

[85] Gregory A. Boyd, *God of the Possible*, p 131

and matter is evil and that only the world of pure spirit is good, so that a world without evil would be a world of disembodied spirits sitting on non-spatio-temporal clouds playing non-physical harps. Imagining that is certainly not easy. Fortunately it is not what we are called upon to do.'[86] In contrast, 'the central Christian affirmation is that what the creator God has done in Jesus Christ, and supremely in his resurrection, is what he intends to do for the whole world – meaning, by 'world', the entire cosmos with all its history.'[87] The reference to God as creator is unmissable. We are about to discover that God's nature and methods in creation can help us to understand a little of his nature and methods in dealing with evil.

However, perhaps the parallel between Jewish, early Christian and Greek thought is not quite the whole of the story. We are so familiar with the narrative nature of much of the Old Testament that it's easy to miss how new and different that was. The Israelites understood their mission to be to affirm that there was one God (hence, of course, the first Commandment) and that he was their leader out of the past, through the present, and into the future. This was in complete contrast to the surrounding tribes and cultures which in general believed that life was an endless repeat – the same thing would come round again and again. If no direction, no history. From this radical Jewish insight we get not only a sense of history, but an idea of the companionship of God and the direction of time, as well as the possibility of doing science, and the whole narrative nature of music. And doubtless more that I haven't thought of! Interestingly enough, in a later section we will consider some aspects of science and music rather in the same breath.

Meanwhile, we can be encouraged that our Jewish heritage

[86] N.T. Wright, *Evil and the Justice of God*, p 67
[87] Tom Wright, *Surprised by Hope*, p 103

leads us to a God who is involved with 'now', and that there-fore heaven is not a motionless 'state of being' but in some way will have its own dynamic. John Polkinghorne puts it like this: 'The life of the new creation will be a temporal life, lived within the unfolding "time" of that world to come, whose everlasting nature is the true meaning of the fulness of times.'[88] For us who ache with the reality of present grief, this entirely ditches the idea of some cosmic weighing machine, in which the bad of the present will be shown to be next to nothing compared to the weight of future glory. And we need to be clear: when Paul speaks in Rom 8:18 about 'our present sufferings' not being 'worth comparing with the glory that will be revealed in us', he is talking about suffering because of being a Christian – an all too present reality for his readers – and not the sufferings that come with being a member of the human race.

For the sake of balance, we should note that in some other respects it was possible for early Christian thinkers and writers to take some of Plato's thought and show that while it was good as far as it went, Christianity was able to bring it to fulfil-ment. In particular, Plato 'ascribed particular importance to ... the notion of the *logos* (Greek: 'word') through which the rationality of the world is communicated and conceptu-alised.'[89] This idea would have been well known to John and his readers for instance, when he opened his Gospel with the declaration 'In the beginning was the Word' (Jn 1:1). But the new and shocking claim is that the *logos* is personal, and can be known. Later, at the end of the second century, Clement of Alexandria 'simultaneously builds his thinking on Platonic ideas, while at the same time stressing the inadequacy of the philosophical system in comparison with Christianity ...

---

[88] John Polkinghorne, *Exploring Reality*, p 125
[89] Alister McGrath, *Christian Theology*, Blackwell Publishing 2007, p 176

(which) speaks and knows of the *logos* incarnate – and hence available and displayed to human sight.'[90] So it wasn't all bad – but a static heaven caught in some kind of celestial amber never had a place in a Christianity that had its roots in Jewish thought.

***

That was Plato. Now we'd better take a moment to see off the Victorians, or at least the Victorian hymn-writers, with their appeal to a heavenly pseudo-comfort which is no comfort at all. This is more serious than taking easy pot-shots at senti-mental second-rate poets who at least meant well. Their thinking, so deeply influenced by the Christian tradition of making an accommodation with Plato, has sunk far into casual Christian thinking, even if the hymns themselves are going out of fashion. We need to see this mind-set for what it is and clear our heads of it, if we are to have a chance of putting the bad stuff in a proper context.

In a society where the children of the unimaginably poor were sent up the chimneys of the unforgivably rich, it was always going to be easier to offer '*a home for little children above the bright blue sky*' than to address matters of justice and human dignity. But at the distance we now are from that society, and certainly remembering that there will be things about our own times to which we are blind, it's not difficult to see the hideous results of projecting all one's hopes for the righting of wrongs onto some future instantly-perfected exis-tence, unconnected to what went before. This leads inevitably to the following miserable bit of philosophy:

---

[90] Ibid., p 177

The trials that beset you, the sorrows ye endure,
the manifold temptations that death alone can cure,

what are they but his jewels of right celestial worth?
what are they but the ladder set up to heaven on earth?

O happy band of pilgrims, look upward to the skies,
Where such a light affliction shall win so great a prize.

If J.M. Neale's offering is an accurate picture of Christianity's answer to our pain, then let's be done with it, eat, drink and be merry, for tomorrow we die. And what Christmas would be complete without at least one rendition of Mrs Alexander's *Once in Royal David's city*?

Not in that poor lowly stable,
with the oxen standing by,
we shall see him; but in heaven,
set at God's right hand on high;
where like stars his children crowned
all in white shall wait around.

No surprise that it's the children again who are being offered jam tomorrow, as the White Queen offered to Alice in Lewis Carroll's *Through the Looking Glass*. And more reinforcement of a static and terrifyingly boring heaven. No: none of this will do. Either Christianity has something more gritty and honest to say about our subject, or we'd better look elsewhere, or give up.

But I don't think we need to despair. We have not been wasting our time. 'Re-emphasising the doctrine of creation is … the foundation of all biblical answers to questions about who God is and what he is doing.'[91] I think we can begin to see some glimmerings, not of a 'solution' of course, for that would

[91] N.T. Wright, *Evil and the Justice of God*, p 41

be naïve, but of a way in which we might find a reason not to give up on faith in a loving God – no more than that. It all comes back to understanding both the nature of the created order, and the nature of creativity itself. The creator shows us his character through the way he creates and sustains; then that same creator becomes *Logos* incarnate. And dies. We noted earlier that in Colossians 1:16 Paul says, 'All things were created by him and for him' and he finishes with the affirmation that he made 'peace through his blood, shed on the cross' (v 20). Let's not rush to judgement over just what that 'peace' might be, but we know what our hearts tell us we need. If we could find that he speaks with one voice in these apparently different areas of creation and peacemaking, we might just be onto something.

As I began writing this, I thought it was going to be about finding an answer to evil. As we have gone on, it has turned out to be more an investigation into creation, the nature of creativity, the nature of God, and something about the way he does things. If we could understand creativity and the creative process, we might then have a place, a context, into which each of us can put his or her story. So the next and final stage of our journey before attempting some conclusions is to look at human creativity, in the hope that it may shed some light on God's.

Four

FINDING GOD IN THE DARK

MADE TO BE MAKERS

> *God be in my head,*
>   *and in my understanding;*
>
> *God be in mine eyes,*
>   *and in my looking;*
>
> *God be in my mouth,*
>   *and in my speaking;*
>
> *God be in my heart,*
>   *and in my thinking;*
>
> *God be at mine end,*
>   *and at my departing.*

(Pynson's *Horae*, 1514)

I don't know whether I like it, but it's what I meant.

(Vaughan Williams on his 4th Symphony)

A few years ago, the institution where I teach aspiring professional musicians took it upon itself to go through a 'restructuring'. This was Newspeak for threatening a number of teaching staff with redundancy. Myself included. Now of course this is something that many employees are faced with, and to some extent it's a fact of commercial life. But it certainly seemed out of place and shocking in a non-commercial, artistic environment. For a musician or someone involved in one of the other arts, the pursuit of their particular skill, often begun at a very early age, plays a hugely significant part in their identity. It's much more than a job – their art pretty much defines who they are.

I, and all my colleagues who were in the same position,

found this apparent assault on our value and identity as musicians, and therefore as people, extremely hard to deal with. So much so in my case that one day as I arrived to do a day's teaching, much to my surprise and without any forewarning, I fell weeping into the arms of a colleague. I mention this bit of autobiography not to seek sympathy, nor to add this event to the list of the traumas that have led me to re-evaluate and redefine my Christian belief, and certainly not to suggest that this event was at all on the same level as those – yours or mine. It is what happened immediately afterwards that will, I hope, serve as a useful backdrop for this next part of our enquiry. First of all, my colleague sent me straight off to talk to the resident Counsellor. This was the first of numerous sessions in which we explored what it means for events to be outside one's personal control. In the context of my life as a musician, first as a performer and later as a teacher, this gave me some very important insights about the loss of control that goes with any creative undertaking, and I will draw out some of those ideas in a moment. The other, more immediate, piece of advice I was given was to go home via an art gallery. So it was that not many minutes later I found myself spending some time contemplating two or three Impressionist paintings in the National Gallery, and then sitting quietly for a while in the beautiful and calming space of the church of St Martin-in-the-Fields.

This was a vivid and timely illustration of what I suppose is no more than a truism: that art in general connects with us at the very deepest level, beyond the place where words have anything useful to contribute. (And, as we come to this last section of a book that has – how could it be otherwise? – involved a lot of words, it's worth remembering that silence may be not just an appropriate response to the suffering of ourselves or others, but something that actually permits and promotes the healing of body and mind.) We instinctively know, though, that art or music that is merely pretty is not what we need. 'Pretty' might be enough to decorate our bedroom or amuse us with some catchy tunes; but the stuff that really works, that meets us beyond words, is grittier than that. And why might that be? It seems to me that only art that is produced under some kind of pressure, or out of some kind of conflict, will do the trick. And that means that the creator must at some stage have had some kind of trouble with it.

[We should be careful here, particularly in the context of thinking of God as creator: the 'trouble' does not arise from the material being in some way second-rate or even opposed to the creator, but is simply a factor of its 'otherness'. In this exploration of issues that take place within the physical environment that we inhabit, we must avoid any idea that the physical world is some kind of mistake, or unworthy of having been created and being sustained by the one God. The Council of Nicea in 325 explicitly rejected this idea of dualism, whereby the 'physical' was thought to be inferior to the 'spiritual'. However, the idea is still alive and well today, though often in shadowy form, as the background to plenty of Christian thought. And it's easy to see the link between this thought and the Platonic idea of static perfection that we dealt with towards the end of the previous chapter. As I said there, God 'seems to do physicality'. This perhaps expresses, though in less comprehensive and certainly less elegant language, something of what the beginning of the Nicene Creed is trying to convey: 'We believe in one God, the Father, the Almighty, maker of heaven and earth, of all that is, seen and unseen.' This is the universe God meant. However, it remains the case that a mark of true creativity is the difficulty that may be encountered in bringing the thing to completion.]

The trouble that the human creator has may simply be the

pain of bringing the piece of work to birth. It may be that the material from which it has to be made is unyielding or unpromising. It may be that the subject matter is painful to face up to. But whatever the particular detail may be, the artist, the composer, the poet has not been the unthinking recipient and passer-on of something that came into his or her head fully formed. It took work, and active thought, and probably many an unsuccessful excursion before the thing was 'finished'.[92]

What does this mean for the person doing the creating? The first thing, paradoxically, is a **loss of control**. We might have thought that the artist was exactly trying to *impose* control on his material. But I think it's more accurate to think of the process as 'encouraging the material to become ordered' – and that is a very different kind of event. In some way the material – whether words or notes or paint – must be allowed to find its own way. Technique will guide this, of course, for there is no human creativity without learned skill and exercised discipline. But ultimately the creator can't say exactly how it will turn out until it's done. W.H. Vanstone describes this beautifully, imagining a painter or poet at work: 'There comes the moment of the bold brushstroke or the adventurous

---

[92] My thoughts in the following section (and my wider thinking) owe a considerable amount to W.H. Vanstone's wonderful meditation on the nature of love from which I quoted in an earlier chapter. He attempts to understand love through considering a number of characteristics which would indicate that something was a false example of love; and thence to come to some idea about its nature when found in authentic form. 'From these,' he says, 'we may approximate to a description of authentic love as limitless, as precarious and as vulnerable.' (*Love's Endeavour, Love's Expense*, p 53.) It is clear that there is an intimate connection between these flavours of love, and aspects of the nature of the creative process.

image ... We see, at the moment of lost control, the most intense endeavour of the artist: and his greatness lies in his ability to discover ever-new reserves of power to meet each challenge of precarious adventure – each challenge of powers exceeded and of control lost.'[93] If the work is successful, then in the finished product we will not see the agonies that the artist went through when it seemed that it might end in failure. But without those moments of loss of control it might have remained merely pretty, rather than achieving beauty.

And when it is done, then what? Maybe people won't like it. The history of music is littered with works which are now accepted as masterpieces, but which were either forgotten soon after the first performance, or even rejected out of hand. The first performance of Stravinsky's ballet *The Rite of Spring* in Paris in 1913 famously provoked a riot between members of the audience who took up violently opposing views as to its merits. It is possible in fact that the catalyst may have had more to do with Nijinsky's choreography than with Stravinsky's music. But whichever it was, it seems that something else that comes as standard with the creative process is an **acceptance of vulnerability.** There are no guarantees.

On that day in the National Gallery I turned instinctively to paintings by Monet and Pissarro – some of the 'Impressionists'. They certainly helped to calm my anger and distress, and reminded me of the beauty of the natural world that exists to some extent independently of any crisis in my circumstances. Somehow the view from inside the artist's head helped me towards the glimmerings of a sense of perspective. Yet the label of 'Impressionist' that we are all familiar with is not quite as straightforward as it appears. The movement that eventually led to Impressionism had started in 1863 when works by

---

[93] W.H. Vanstone, *Love's Endeavour, Love's Expense*, p 48

Cézanne, Manet, Pissarro and others were exhibited at the 'Salon des Refusés', having been rejected for exhibition in the Salon proper. Manet's now famous 'Déjeuner sur l'herbe' caused a sensation. These and other artists continued to develop their new style which often focused on painting 'direct' in the open air, and on capturing the ephemeral effects of changing light. Then in 1874 at the first exhibition of the newly formed 'Societé Anonyme des Artistes' Monet exhibited his 'Impression, soleil levant' – 'Impression, sunrise'. The contemporary critic Louis Leroy saw a journalistic opportunity and coined the label 'Impressionist' as a sarcastic term of abuse. (Not for the first or last time, a critic is remembered mainly for being wrong.) So works of art that we now couldn't imagine being deprived of were originally greeted with resistance or incomprehension or downright rejection. There is an echo here of an idea that we touched on before: that God, in the context of his creation experiment, may be capable of experiencing regret, loss, and (as yet) unfulfilled desire.

I referred earlier to the notebooks of Beethoven, which are notoriously difficult to decipher. This doesn't matter at all, as they were entirely linked to his creative process, and produced doubtless with no thought or concern that one day scholars would pore over them and write learned articles about them. But what is clear from even a casual look at them is that the material that we now know so well and that seems so inevitable often started out quite differently, and the finished product was achieved through continual testing and trying and refining. So the composer has to permit an **openness to unexpected possibilities**. Far from implying a lack of skill or foresight, this mindset, dangerous though it is, turns out to be the only path towards creating something that is genuinely 'other' than its creator. Until the thing is done no one, not even the composer, can say exactly how it's going to turn out.

It seems to me that this state of affairs is necessary in order to give due weight to the identity of the material, and to treat it with the honour it deserves as an external entity. We could note the rather obvious parallel that will be familiar to anyone who has brought up children, or taught them, or in other ways had responsibility for them. Whatever there may have been of nature and of nurture, those two elements by themselves, even if we knew all that there was to know about every influence, could never fully predict what a child will become. If we are to give proper value to the child as a unique individual, there will be aspects of his or her development over which those who exercise some influence have no control. To behave and believe otherwise would be to deny the independent person-hood of the child, and would limit the possibility of their growth to maturity.

This idea of openness to unexpected possibilities should not be taken to imply any kind of passivity on the part of the cre-ative artist. These possibilities may be unexpected, but they are unlikely to appear fully formed, of their own volition. They have to be teased out, even if once they are in place it may seem impossible that they could ever have been absent. I think the experience of writing, and particularly of writing poetry, is probably like that. Language has to be pressed into service, made to do things it usually doesn't, and new connections have to be made in order to say something original. It is thought that Shakespeare may have added as many as two thousand words or phrases to the English language, or at least ensured their long-term currency. You may feel that in some of what I have tried to put across so far, I have worn my heart upon my sleeve. Well, if so, and if we all know what I mean by that, then we have Shakespeare (in Othello) to thank for this vivid image which is now part of the language. It takes a genius who can find unexpected possibilities in previously unconnected words to take a part of the body and an article of clothing and, by uniting them, say something that we now feel could not be said so well any other way. The possibility of marrying the two concepts was unexpected, and had to be discovered by searching.

A little nearer our own times, we could think of that alchemist of language Gerard Manley Hopkins. He too sought out possibilities in surprising connections, in order to express his wonder at the created world. His well-known 'Hurrahing in Harvest' begins

> *Summer ends now; barbarous in beauty, the stooks rise*
> *Around; up above, what wind-walks! what lovely behaviour*
> *Of silk-sack clouds! has wilder, wilful-wavier*
> *Meal-drift moulded ever and melted across skies?*[94]

The possibilities of these combinations add up to far more than the sum of their parts. They are surprising, but enlightening, to us, and perhaps were surprising to Gerard Manley Hopkins too.

[This discussion of some aspects of creativity has of course focused on the arts. But in fact there is a sense in which the scientific process is creative too. The history of science can be seen as the business of finding a theory that would make sense of surprising facts. Darwin's theory of natural selection, for instance, seemed to have a better 'fit' with his intimate observations of the natural world than explanations that proposed a once-for-all creation where everything came into being fully formed and at the same time. The scientist must be open to, and indeed searches out, unexpected possibilities. As for an acceptance of vulnerability, that would at first sight seem to be far from the rather precise world of the scientist. But not every

---

[94] Gerard Manley Hopkins, *Poems and Prose*, Penguin Classics, first publ. 1953, p 31

new idea is greeted with acclamation even within the scientific community itself. A relatively recent example is the coining by Sir Fred Hoyle of the term 'the Big Bang', which has echoes of the first use of the word Impressionism as described above. Hoyle used this phrase in a radio broadcast in 1949 to distinguish this theory of the origin of the universe from his own 'Steady State' proposal. Hoyle's idea has now been discredited, but whilst he continued to reject the Big Bang theory for the rest of his life, the name stuck and is now the label for the universally accepted description of how the universe came to be.]

These three elements of the creative process, then – loss of control, acceptance of vulnerability and openness to unexpected possibilities - all add up to the fact that **creativity costs.** And the cost is paid not just by the creator, but by innocent bystanders as well. Hilary Spurling gives a vivid account of what Henri Matisse (and those near him, not least his model Lisette) went through before his monumental work 'The Dance' was completed. The work had been commissioned by millionaire collector Dr Albert C. Barnes, to adorn the entrance hall of his new museum in Philadelphia. The description is worth quoting at some length.

'Lisette was forbidden to swim except briefly, first thing in the morning, for fear of sunburn. Once she was battered by a freak wave and came home badly bruised, only to be reprimanded for spoiling the immaculate purity Matisse needed for his work. It required long hours, short breaks and exclusive concentration from both painter and model. After six months, *The Dance* was no longer flowing as smoothly as its creator had anticipated. An old friend, the painter Georges Desvallières, was frankly appalled. "He is working himself to death on imperceptible changes that bring others in their wake, which he may think better of the next day." Whenever panic loomed in Nice, Bussy (an old friend of the artist) received a telegram: DECORATION IN TERRIBLE STATE COMPOSITION COMPLETELY OUT OF HAND AM IN DESPAIR LIGHT SUITABLE THIS AFTERNOON FOR GODS SAKE COME AT ONCE MATISSE. Throughout the long slow evolution of *The Dance* Bussy regularly arrived to find his old comrade fraught and frantic ("struggling with his vast composition like a kitten with an outsize ball of wool" wrote Bussy's daughter, Janie. "The great dim monstrous de-individualised figures he had conceived began to wind themselves into impossible knots."). Barnes's decoration was nearing completion more or less on time and the American press was already preparing a noisy reception for it when Matisse made the horrible discovery that he had been working for 12 months from measurements miscalculated by almost a metre.'[95]

Graham Greene takes this idea of the cost to others of someone's creativity and puts it in the mouth of Henry Pulling, the world-weary bank manager narrator of *Travels with my Aunt*. 'I had once read, in a book on Charles Dickens, that an author must not be attached to his characters, he must treat them without mercy. In the act of creation there is always, it seems, an awful selfishness. So Dickens's wife and mistress had to suffer so that Dickens could make his novels and his fortune. At least a bank manager's money is not so tainted by egotism. Mine was not a destructive profession. A bank manager doesn't leave a trail of the martyred behind him.'[96] This last

[95] Hilary Spurling, *Matisse the Master; a Life of Henri Matisse 1909–1954* Penguin paperback, 2006. [Quoted in The Times Online book review, January 27th 2006]

[96] Graham Greene, *Travels with my Aunt*, Vintage, 1999, p 22

sentence clearly predates the banking crisis of recent years! Even on its own terms it is a rather jaundiced and certainly earth-centred view of the cost of creativity, and we would be wise not to stretch it too far for anything that it might be able tell us about the creativity that God has involved us in. But the point remains: there is a cost to those who did not ask to be involved in the project.

To complete this brief look at creativity, we need to add one more factor which applies to 'performed' arts in general, and to music in particular. It's so obvious that one could miss it: **music has to be performed by people**! So far we have been thinking – to continue with the example of music – about the process that results in the existence of the composer's score, when the sounds imagined in the creative mind of the composer have been notated into a form in which they can be conveyed to anyone who can read music. But the written score is not the piece! It's merely the means whereby the piece can come to be performed. And what happens when it receives a number of performances? Are they all the same? Well – yes, and no. One of the tasks of a performer, and indeed of the teacher who tries to guide the development of young performers, is to seek the most detailed faithfulness possible to the written notes, but also, and simultaneously, to seek a reading of the work that is unique to that performer. Otherwise, of course, the best performances would be those programmed into a computer, whereas in reality one would so much rather have a performance with a few wrong notes but a personal and faithful response to the score.

On a recent visit to a rather splendid science museum in Ironbridge, cradle of the industrial revolution, I was surprised to hear some piano music drifting across the exhibits. As I followed the sound to its source, it turned out to be coming from a beautifully restored 'player piano', where the notes of the score are translated into small holes in a rotating roll of paper, and thence by a rather complicated and miraculous mechanical system are made to depress the keys of the piano. It was playing the last movement of Beethoven's 'Moonlight Sonata', which was quite a good choice for demonstrating the wonders of this long-superseded bit of kit, as it's full of arpeggios up the length of the keyboard, and plenty of contrast of dynamic. To begin with it was amusing and interesting, and it drew quite a crowd. But after a while, as it began a second, and then a third, and a fourth, performance, it began to be irritating and even rather disturbing, to me at least! It became possible to predict exactly how it would play the next phrase, and that kind of certainty about what was to come, linked to the knowledge of its non-human production, began to suck the life out of the notes I was hearing, making them into only the most superficial account of the piece.

For myself, I have an unfashionable dislike for listening to recordings even when made by a real person. Give me the spontaneity of a live performance any day. Occasionally a student will tell me that they have been listening to a recording of mine, and I take a slightly malicious pleasure in responding to any compliment with 'Yes, I wish I could play like that' – since almost all recordings are made up of the best bits from numerous attempts. Digital recording has made this the simplest of processes. In a live performance you only get one go.

The same point could be made of course about any of the performing arts. The words of the playwright look definite on the page, and must be correctly delivered if the performance is to be legitimate. But what is 'correctly'? It's far more than making sure that none are added and none are omitted. The performance that the public see is the result of weeks of work by the cast, the director, the set designer and many more, as they try to 'get inside' the words on the page and find a way of understanding the characters and telling the story that will make sense to the audience. Just as with the notes of a musical score, the written words can be delivered in an almost infinite variety of ways. The English language, with its extensive use of intonation, is particularly rich in this respect.

I am no actor, but I remember once having the privilege of reading the first chapter of John's Gospel in a church service. This famous and spirit-lifting passage speaks of Jesus as 'the Word' and describes him as 'full of grace and truth'. Then John says 'For the law was given through Moses; grace and truth came through Jesus Christ.' So here he repeats his earlier reference to Jesus, and to grace and truth. As I thought about how to read this in public, in a way that would bring new light to a perhaps over-familiar passage, it occurred to me that by changing the intonation one could give it two rather different senses. One intonation would emphasise 'through Jesus Christ' and answer the question 'Through whom did that grace and truth come?', whilst the other would emphasise 'grace and truth' and answer the question 'What was it that came through Jesus Christ?' For the record, I decided that the latter was perhaps the more enlightening.

The final performance of a play is, I suppose – though it is also much more than this - the coming together of a vast number of such microscopic moments of decision-making. And, crucially, there is no 'right' answer, but only the one that best fits the performer's conception. In a performing context, that is a definition of integrity.

Finally, in considering the role of the performer, and returning to thinking about music, which I know more about professionally, we should remember that the same artist will play differently on different occasions. Specific factors come into play such as the acoustic of different halls (and, for a pianist, the characteristics of different instruments), as well as less definite ones such as the mood of the moment, or an instinctive response to how the previous phrase just went, or even the performer's sixth sense as to how the audience are reacting and responding to the performance; and in the longer term the imperceptible changes brought about by living with the piece over the course of a career. So what appear to be the definite instructions of the composer turn out to be much less cut and dried than we might have thought.

My teacher Gordon Green used to speak admiringly of the wonder of musical notation. He used to explain how it is specific about things that are specific, notably pitch – the 'what', if you like – but much less exact about other things such as timing – the 'when' – and dynamic and sound quality – the 'how'. All these have to be created by the performer in response – obedience even! – to the first imagination of the composer. In one respect, his point overstated the case for exactness: for pianists, pitch is a 'given', with the intervals between each note – a semitone –unified into identical distances, in the interests of being able to play in any key without some sounding less successful than others. This is the 'equal temperament', to prove the success of which Bach wrote his famous two books of 24 Preludes and Fugues, one in every major and minor key. But for other instruments and, crucially, for a singer (since in one way or another all instruments are seeking to 'sing' according to their different characters) pitch is a matter of judgement. A gloomy or dark word in a song, or a particular 'colour', as musicians say, in a melody or harmony may require the inflection of a note infinitesimally below its 'mean' frequency. Or some other combination of influences will lead the performer to inflect the note slightly sharp. All semitones are created equal, but in practice some are more equal than others. This is all in the hands of the performer, and yet by no means violates the wishes and intentions of the composer. Quite the reverse in fact – this is exactly part of what it means to 'interpret' the piece.

I have occasionally heard teachers say, 'I was teaching such-and-such a piece the other day.' I dislike this casual phrase, with its implication that I will make the same suggestions to any and all students working on it, and the further, rather unpleasant, impression that the way for a student to please me is to play it how I might play it. Perish the thought. The way to artistic maturity is more difficult, for student, teacher and seasoned performer: to find what in the performer's heart and imagination best responds to, and re-creates, the thing first imagined by the composer. The 'great' performance is the one that most perfectly filters the composer's wishes through the sensibility of the performer, and will be full of things I hadn't thought of or seen.

***

So what might these brief thoughts about some aspects of creativity and performance be able to do for us in our search for a creating and redeeming God? Well, no more, but also no less, than offering the possibility of a metaphor. However 'high' (a metaphor!) our view of God, we can only speak of him (a metaphor?) in terms of something or someone we already know about. If there were other language, unconnected to our daily experience, that could be used of God – and there may well be – it would be language unintelligible to humans. It would be appropriate and meaningful only to other beings. We in our few-dimensional existence can speak only of what we know. 'What we know of God is through his relationship to the creation; his involvement with us in that context.'[97] Even in normal conversation we can say very little that is interesting

[97] John Sanders, *The God Who Risks*, Inter-Varsity Press Academic (USA), 2nd edition, 2007, p 29

without using metaphors. 'That performance blew me away.' Not elegant, perhaps, but vivid – in this case, the listening experience as something that comes towards me in a way that I cannot control, and leaves me in a different place from where I began. In fact, talking about music in general requires the extensive use of metaphor, especially in a teaching context, simply because it cannot be touched or seen. So: 'Let that phrase unfold more slowly' – music as something that the performer opens in order to reveal a gift; 'Can you find a brighter colour for that surprising chord?' – music as an experience of seeing and reacting. And so on. And in just the same way we can only speak – and think – of God by using similar means.

John Sanders, in the book I quoted from above, is very helpful here. 'Different models generate different theologies by which God and God's relation to the world are understood. One faith community might focus on God as father while another community emphasises God as king. The first community might develop a patriarchal theology while the latter might develop a hierarchical one. Both would lead to specific forms of church life with rules about how the church should be structured and who should be "at the top".'[98] His book, as the title implies, is about a conception of God for whom the future is open, and not everything is set in stone (a metaphor!) beforehand. This 'open theism' is in contrast to the view known as 'meticulous providence' where God knows everything in advance (from our point of view).

So, just as using the metaphors of father or king will lead to different views of how we should respond to him, so the metaphor of God as Controller will hugely influence how we view the past, the present and the future. Nothing will happen that he does not know about 'in advance' and everything that

---

[98] Ibid., p 26

happens will in some way be what he wants, because his will is never thwarted. This raises huge questions, both philosophical and theological, about what God can be said to be responsible for. Particularly, as we wondered earlier: how blurred is the line between permitting and causing?

But this is not the place to pursue those questions. Our task is more urgent, and I think we can legitimately sidestep these potentially abstruse questions for a good reason. It seems to me that such a picture of God the Controller is anyway no good for those who, because of events in the past – but which were once the terrible present – carry now in this present and into the future the burden of asking the agonised questions like 'Where was God?' and 'Why did he not prevent it?' that we posed in the first chapter. Sanders is explicit about this 'classical theism', as he calls the metaphor of the God of meticulous control. 'The divine nature ascribed to God by classical theism does not allow for God to know what grieving is like or what pain feels like.'[99] In other words he can see these things happening to us but cannot experience them himself. If God can't do better than that, then we're best making our own way through the mess. No: we need a metaphor that fits our facts. 'When God created he did not have a blueprint for everything in creation. Instead, he had a destination in mind and desired to take a journey with us. Both the ultimate goal and the boundaries of the journey are set by the creator, but many of the specifics of the course are set by both God and humans as we travel together in history. Free will theists believe that God is flexible and resourceful in working with us in life.'[100]

The creation project as a journey ... God freely giving up meticulous control ... his openness to future possibilities ...

---

[99] Ibid., p 196
[100] Ibid., p 198 f

his self-imposed need to involve his creatures in the development of the project ... Does all this remind you of anything? We've come right back to our human-angle ideas about creativity. So I want to suggest a metaphor that I think can help us speak intelligibly in our context. I freely acknowledge that it's not one we find explicitly in the Bible, and so it needs to be treated with some care. And of course no metaphor will stretch to say all we want to say. But I think this might shed some light: **God the Composer**.

God's Symphony

If God is the Cosmic Composer, then the whole of the creation project is his Symphony.[101] He knows its general shape, and he knows why he is writing it. We might say that there is a compulsion for him to bring it to completion. This is a way of saying 'Love'. But for it to be a genuine – *the* genuine – work of art, various dangerous things must happen. The material must be allowed to establish its own identity. God must accept a loss of control over the detail. And it will cost him. And his creatures. The God of meticulous control cannot write a symphony.

At this point, since our metaphor is about music, two things need to be said about the nature of music. But this is dangerous territory! Every musician, and every thoughtful listener to music, knows the unwisdom of trying to talk about

---

[101] Alister McGrath in *A Fine-Tuned Universe* has an interesting quote (note, p 84) from Dorothy L. Sayers in her *Letters of a Diminished Church*, Nashville: W Publishing, 2004, p 35-48: 'certain ... difficulties which arise "if one thinks of God as a mechanician" disappear if God is conceived as a "creative artist".' Her endorsement gives me encouragement, if I needed it, to develop my metaphor.

what music 'means'. If we could say in words what music is about, then we would have made the music itself redundant. Whatever it's about, it's expressing things that can be expressed in no other way. That's why we cannot do without it. Every culture knows that. And music can have only that most general, though indispensable, function. The efforts of the Soviet authorities during the communist era to insist on 'socialist realism' from artists, architects and composers are well known, and the extent to which Shostakovich and Prokofiev (to name only the two most prominent Russian composers of the time) did or did not comply has been hotly debated. The only point we need to notice here is that the more overt the propaganda intentions of a work of art, the less likely it is to be regarded by later generations as 'great art'. Its propaganda function inevitably serves to debase its achievement. Great music is not 'for' anything, and not 'about' anything that can be expressed any other way.

But with that proviso I want to draw attention to two aspects of music that have an important bearing on what our metaphor might do for us. The first may be surprising to the non-specialist: a fundamental feature of music (or at least Western music, which is the only sort I am qualified to speak about) is the resolution of discord. The situation since the 20th-century abandonment of tonality is more complex, but up till then – to simplify a fluid and far from homogeneous picture – music was written in keys. The function of the 'home key' – D major, C minor or whatever – was to provide a stable point from which the music would diverge and then finally return, giving a sense of completion. This movement away from the home key is a kind of discord, and is a large-scale version of the small-scale discords that are found in sequences of harmony. These discords could be described as one or more 'wrong' notes added to a plain chord. Scientifically, the effect they produce is a direct result of interference, or complexity, between the various wavelengths of the individual notes. The more complex the relationship between two or more wavelengths, the more there will be a need for resolution onto notes whose wavelengths coincide more readily. The most consonant interval is the octave, where the wavelengths of the two notes are in the relationship 2:1. But for the listener this is not the important point. What matters is the effect. And the effect of a discord is to produce the need for 'resolution' where, usually, the 'wrong' note will fall and take its place as a 'right' note in the next harmony. But, and here is the crucial thing, a piece of music without these discords will be bland and uninteresting. It will not have a sense of direction, since the impression of going forwards in a piece of music is in part a function of the creation and resolution of discord. If no discord, no interest. If no conflict, no sense of achievement and arrival.

A moment ago I said that, for the listener, the science behind discord and resolution in music was not important. This is true on one level: we receive the effect, if that's not too cheap a word, just as powerfully whether or not we know the science. But we are not just listeners. We are also those who are trying to get our heads round the universe, by thinking about philosophy and theology. And for us, I think this science holds an immensely important clue that we can take with us in a search for understanding. If God is the Composer, what kind of music will he write?

As we think about discord it might be objected that the music of a happier world would not need, or produce, this alternating tension and resolution. Perhaps music is only like this because the world it sits in contains all the bad stuff we have been steeling ourselves to look at. Perhaps music simply reflects a skewed world, and has discord because the world doesn't work very well, and has in some deep sense gone wrong. But remember the argument we marshalled earlier, when we were thinking about the 'Fall': the 'given' characteristics of the physical world predate the arrival of humans and whatever glory or mess we have made of things. As there, so here: if wavelengths produce pitch, and some coincide, making concord, whilst others conflict with each other, producing discord, then those characteristics of the way sound is made are built into the foundational mathematics of the universe. It was always so, and music, which is sound turned into art, could never have been otherwise.

Here I take issue with the objection put forward by Jeremy S. Begbie in his contribution to the symposium *The Beauty of God*. In an otherwise enlightening chapter on 'Beauty, Sentimentality and the Arts' he writes about the dangers, as he sees it, of certain theologies that, in an attempt to ' "take suffering seriously"... come close to eternalising evil in God.' He suggests that 'certain British "tragic theologies" ... out of a strong fear of metaphysical optimism, of anything that would trivialize evil, can come close to doing just that through appearing to presume a fundamental, perpetual order of violence and strife in creation, a scenario that arguably encourages something more akin to resignation before the magnitude of evil rather than a revulsion that stems from a confidence born of resurrection faith.'[102] This is a useful corrective, perhaps, but I maintain that the sequence of tension, or discord, followed by resolution, is built into the fabric of the aural world in general and of music in particular, in a way that surely predates whatever mess humans may have made of God's world. And this leads us directly to the second aspect of music that we need to

---

[102] Jeremy S. Begbie in *The Beauty of God. Theology and the Arts*, ed. Daniel J. Treier, Mark Husbands and Roger Lundin, InterVarsity Press, 2007, pp 66, 67

bear in mind.

If that was a technical characteristic of music that has a bearing on the picture we are trying to draw, the other element is more to do with its power to engage our emotions. Emotion is of course a hugely important fact of life for a musician, and one that a performer must have the courage to embrace and engage with. Amongst the many short piano pieces that Brahms wrote towards the end of his life is his Intermezzo Op 117/3 in C# minor. It was written in 1892, just five years before his death. It's a gentle, rather private piece, understated but full of rich harmony and searching melody, reaching no big climax, and saving its most poignant phrase for the end. Of this short but great work Brahms said that it was 'the lullaby of all my griefs'. But, as we respond to its emotional potency, should we say that this wonderful piece is unutterably beautiful or unbearably sad? The answer is 'Yes'. And we could give the same answer if the adjectives were the other way round: 'Is this unbearably beautiful or unutterably sad?' One way or the other, it seems to be the case that in music there is no clear distinction between beauty and sadness. We should note, though, that this is not the same as beginning to talk about what music 'means'. As we have seen already, if we could say what it means, we wouldn't need the music. It is what it is, of itself, and can't be expressed in any other way. But the parts of us that respond to it are identifiable, so we are aware when it connects to whatever we know of beauty, and of sadness, and in our experience it turns out that we can't easily distinguish between the two.

It's rather like the often-observed fact that a particular smell may trigger a long-forgotten memory, with the result that we can hardly tell which came first, and which is the more vivid – the memory of the event, or the memory of the smell. In this case it seems that the cause is the physical proximity in the brain of the centres dealing with smell and memory. But in the case of music – its ability to enable us to respond to beauty and our finding it makes us sad, or to enable us to respond to sadness and our finding it is beautiful – I am sure that the 'cause', if that's not too prosaic a word, of this mixing is not mechanical, or at least not exclusively mechanical. It is not merely a matter of brain function. This quality in music is pointing us to something profound about the nature of existence. Apart from theology, it's perhaps the best mirror we have.

In a chapter by Roger Lundin from the book I quoted above, he observes that this idea is found also in the writings of Karl Barth, and particularly in his *Ethics*. 'Along with humor, art is an activity of which "only the children of God are capable," and, like humor, it is "born of sorrow" and "sustained by an ultimate and very profound pain." '[103] Jeremy S. Begbie observes in his chapter that 'a constant remembrance (*anamnesis*) of the cross will prevent the pleasure that rightly attends beauty from sliding into sentimentality, for beauty at its richest has been forged through the starkness and desolation of Good Friday: indeed, as the Revelation to St John reminds us, the risen Lamb on the throne bears the marks of suffering (Rev 5:6).'[104] Absolutely, and we must not forget this essential perspective. But I would want to go back a step or two and suggest again that if beauty and sadness are linked in some way at the cross, then we can also dimly see that the salvation-event inaugurated by the incarnation is in some deep way attached to more than 'just' our need of salvation from sin. The very nature of the created order brings with it an agony and a potential for grief that God perhaps always knew he must address. We will look at this idea more closely in the next chapter.

---

[103] Ibid., p 207, quoting Karl Barth *Ethics*, ed. Dietrich Braun, trans. Geoffrey W. Bromiley, New York: Seabury, 1981, pp 506, 507

[104] Ibid., p 64

So those two aspects of music, the inevitability of discord, with its need for resolution, and the indivisibility of beauty and sadness, can perhaps give us a clue about the kind of music that God is writing. But who is performing this symphony? Well, it seems clear that if God is the composer, then we are the orchestra. We have that freedom-within-discipline to interpret the work, to bring to it our own unique sensibility. We are the ones who can bring the work to life. Our best performance will be the one in which we are able to be utterly faithful to the score, but also to be fully and honestly our unique selves. The general plan is clear, but the detail will depend on the beauty of the sound that each of us is able to make. God needs the players, or his composition will remain unheard.

This is not quite the whole story though. There is another hugely important figure involved in the performance. Behold the conductor, that mysterious figure who can inspire or infuriate an orchestra. His job is to bring out the best in the players and achieve cohesion out of what would otherwise be a free-for-all cacophony. Now, there are conductors and conductors. Musicians are inclined to take a rather jaundiced view of the difference between a great and a poor conductor: with the latter they get on best by taking as little notice as possible and pooling their collective skills and experience with minimal, or less, reference to the conductor; whereas the great conductor is the one who can inspire them to play to the limits of their skill, and perhaps beyond. With a great conductor there is a kind of alchemy at work. Although technique is involved, and specific indications need to be given to the players, the process is fundamentally one where music is drawn out from them, rather than being imposed upon them. They have freedom, but it is a freedom to do what the conductor is imagining. And of course his imagination is guided by the wishes of the composer.

But there is a further twist to the story in our case of God the composer: the conductor and the composer are one and the same. He has come to take part in the performance. He hasn't just left us the score – the instructions – but having made himself vulnerable by the very act of creating, he has pursued that vulnerability to the point of taking part with us in the performance. Though as composer he knows and understands the work in a way that we cannot, yet as conductor he has come right into it with us. He shares all his knowledge and understanding and inspiration with us, but he cannot perform his Symphony without us. We are all in this together.

We observed earlier that our search for answers had become much less a question of 'How can I understand the bad stuff?' and much more a question of 'Where can I put it?' At that point we were able to say, 'In the only world there could ever have been – but in a world that will be transformed and redeemed.' With the backdrop of the thoughts we have just been exploring about the nature of creativity and of music, and God's activity as composer and conductor of his great Creation Symphony, we can – at last! – turn to see how these ideas might help us take hold of the incarnation, life, death and resurrection of Jesus. If we are to find healing anywhere, it will be here, in the music that God has written – is writing – and in the fact of his joining with us in the performance. His music, our music together, will have discord and resolution, and sadness and beauty will sing the same tune.

GOD'S MUSIC

If you ain't lived it, it won't come out your horn.

(attributed to saxophonist Charlie Parker)

Nur wer die Sehnsucht kennt,
Weiss, was ich leide!
Only the one who has experienced longing
Can know what I am suffering!

(Goethe)

If this journey that we have been on together were to conclude in terms of an explanation of a problem, or an answer
to a question, or the solution of a difficulty, you would say that
it can't possibly be as tidy as that, and that I had led you to this
point only to offer something that was too definite to have
about it the ring of truth. And you would be right. Where
philosophers and theologians, and the biblical writers themselves, have in their different ways said that words will ultimately have to fall silent, and understanding will have to defer
to patience, it's unlikely that the thoughts of one more
wounded and bewildered Christian will suddenly come up
with something that no one else has thought of. But I hope that
what we have found in the previous chapters is – how to put it?
– a kind of language to use, and a context in which to speak it.

I referred at the end of the previous chapter to the incarnation, life, death and resurrection of Jesus. These are of course
the chief staging-posts in that rather splendid progression that
we call the Christian Year. It is splendid partly because it's a
wonderful guard against a lack of balance. It ensures that we
don't emphasise one element at the expense of another. And it
roots our belief in God's historical action. This is all good. But
there is a possible downside as well. It can lead us, if we're not

careful, to put the different stages into separate compartments, and perhaps miss the point that the whole story is indeed one story. If God is joining us in the performance of his Symphony, then the sequence of (historical) events that we follow in the Christian Year is like the sequence of events that we follow in a piece of music. Each only makes sense in the context of the whole. (And let's not forget that the performance isn't finished yet!) So the following concluding thoughts are an attempt to find a way of saying something about God's creation-project-performance in the light simultaneously of what we have discovered about creation and creativity and of what we could think of as that part of the performance where God appears as composer-conductor. It's all one piece. As we begin this, I want first to see if our thoughts so far can throw some new and perhaps surprising light on a familiar Christian idea.

   '**Forgiving God.**' English is an unusual language in its lack of case-endings and the normally simple shapes of its verb conjugations. This is why it lends itself to crosswords in a way that many other languages don't. Less pleasingly, the plasticity of English also permits the ungainliness of the newspaper vendor's headline like the apocryphal 'Death Plunge Man Trial Verdict Sensation'. More seriously, the heading of this paragraph could mean either of two things: 'forgiving' can be an adjectival usage, so 'a God whose character is that of one who forgives', or it can be a verb proper, so 'telling God that we forgive him'. We are well used to the first one, but I want to consider this second, more surprising, way of reading it.

   Now, we must be careful what we mean. The two directions of forgiveness cannot be quite the same. God has not sinned against me or against his creation in the way in which I have sinned against him. He is God and can legitimately make demands of behaviour on me. If, as I do, I fail to meet those demands, it is appropriate that I incur some kind of disapproval. (I am deliberately trying not to use religious language in order to keep the sequence of thought as clean as possible.) God is God and must be allowed to be so. And yet, and yet ... Part of what we have been exploring has been the over-whelming sensation that God has not lived up to expectations, not in moral behaviour but rather in the exercise of power and authority over events, and this has led to a depth of disap-pointment and anger which I have tried to express honestly but also with some restraint. It has been about a world where what happened can happen.

So as long as we are careful what we mean, I think it is legit-imate to have the idea that maybe God can ask – and receive – forgiveness for the precariousness and cost of his Creation project, his great Symphony, the making and performing of which is so costly to all who are involved. By creating, he has voluntarily and purposely given up meticulous control over the material, and allowed it to be open to new possibilities. He has made himself vulnerable – to the point of death – as he takes part with us in the performance, and the language of cre-ation's music contains in its very DNA the mixing of beauty and grief. The creation project is certainly a costly under-taking, and we're in it whether we like it or not. Perhaps by exercising forgiveness in the sense I have been describing we can begin to come to terms with the way the world is.

In a broadcast interview, The Archbishop of Canterbury, Rowan Williams, made the helpful and important point that to forgive means having faith in the person forgiven. Forgiveness and faith are inextricably linked – opposite sides of the same coin. Abandoned on the cross, Jesus prayed for his persecutors to be forgiven. And let us not miss the perhaps shocking truth that there is no waiting for them to act in any way. They do not have to repent before they can come to God for forgiveness. God is apparently able to forgive unilaterally. God's trust is, unbelievably, in them. As far as we can tell it is not a matter of theirs in him.

But in more mundane circumstances too we can easily see the inextricable tie-up between trust and forgiveness. If a parent forgives a child, it is not because the offence is deemed to be no offence, but because the parent is expressing faith in the possibility of the child's development into one who behaves better. Or if one member of a couple is unfaithful, there are basically two options. Either the aggrieved party says, 'I cannot trust you any more,' and the scene is set perhaps for the breakdown of the relationship; or they may say, 'In spite of what has happened, I trust you enough to go on working at our relationship.' It can perhaps be 'redeemed', and then the expression of trust is the same as the offer of forgiveness, or at least enables the process of forgiving to begin. There is a third option, in fact, where the couple live on 'together' but not really together, in an atmosphere of mutual recrimination and distrust. This is not an honest or viable response to the event, and as I said right at the beginning, it is to avoid the equivalent of that in my relationship with God that I have embarked on this voyage. So whilst it is true that 'I must trust God in order to be forgiven', it may also be true that 'I must trust God in order to forgive him'. The forgiveness by a parent or a partner are expressions not just of trust, but of enduring and unconditional love, and so it is with God. 'His forgiveness' is directed by his love; and 'his forgiveness' in the other sense can be the way I acknowledge that love for him is not lost. Forgiving is what love does. A father who lost a child in the 9/11 terrorist attack later sought out the mother of one of the hijackers in order to understand, and thereby to seek to forgive. This is costly love that can heal.

And we'd better get the hang of it. 'Not to forgive,' says Tom Wright, 'is to shut down a faculty in the innermost person, which happens to be the same faculty that can receive God's forgiveness. It also happens to be the same faculty that can experience real joy and real grief. Love bears all things, believes all things, hopes all things, endures all things.'[105] He is speaking of forgiving others, but I think the principle applies equally to our direct relationship with God. If I cannot forgive him, maybe I cannot be forgiven. If I cannot forgive him, maybe I slowly die.

To return to the event which was the focal point of the coming of Christ, we are used to hearing that 'the cross' is God's answer. But what is the question? The sticking point for us, I have suggested, is not some overwhelming sense of our own sinfulness and unworthiness, though that will doubtless never be far away, but a profound awareness of the cost of the creation project. I have been arguing that the world is as it is, and could not be otherwise. We cannot ask for a different Symphony to be performed. So, with respect, due deference and plenty of awareness of our mere creatureliness, could it be that God's action in Christ's incarnation-life-death is his way of asking our forgiveness? The least he could do was all he could do – be part of it with us. Given that the creation project is up and running, he has at least taken part with us. We have no choice but to be in it. He did have that choice, but chose to be in it anyway. There was no more that he could do, and perhaps by virtue of that we can find it in our hearts to forgive him, and decide to make our music – his music – together with him. This is a dangerous thought, and I repeat that we must in the same breath acknowledge that he and we do not speak as equals. If to be a creating God means anything, his creatures are just that: separate, and owing their entire existence to him.

---

[105] Tom Wright, *Surprised by Hope*, p 301

We are not Gods. But God has become one of us and *asks our forgiveness*. Dare we think it? Dare we do it? This whole investigation has been a huge risk, so we might as well go on taking risks to the end. Nothing ventured in this case, certainly nothing gained. I risk the idea and I risk the action. God have mercy on me and on you.

But we must not miss the further event beyond the incarnation-life-death sequence, which is of course the resurrection of Jesus. It turned the disciples from frightened and disappointed former-followers into amazed proclaimers of the fact that we have entered – begun to play! – the Prelude to the Part Two which will be the climax of the Symphony. If the resurrection is the turning-point in the argument of the Symphony, what can be its significance for the broken-hearted, whom Psalm 147:3 tells us that God heals, and whose wounds he binds up? Not what we were taught to think, I suggest.

It's surprising that Tom Wright's book from which I just quoted has not caused more of a stir. 'Bishop of Durham casts doubt on meaning of resurrection' is the kind of headline that became familiar during the time of his predecessor, David Jenkins. This is not the place to reopen that debate, but listen to Tom Wright: 'The resurrection stories in the gospels *aren't about going to heaven when you die* [his italics]. In fact, there is almost nothing about "going to heaven when you die" in the whole New Testament.' His position is a million miles away from Jenkins', but equally radical – more so, perhaps. 'Jesus' resurrection is the beginning of God's new project, not to snatch people away from earth to heaven, but to colonize earth with the life of heaven.'[106] The burden of his book is that we are destined not for a disembodied heaven, but for a redeemed

---

[106] Ibid., p 305

new heaven *and* new earth. This new earth will be physical, but not subject to decay. Or, as we might put it, Jesus' resurrection is the music of the opening pages of the Prelude to Part Two, and it sets out the material (in at least two senses) that will form the glorious music of the Symphony's climax. The resurrection appearances of Jesus were the breaking through of the new physicality into the time-frame of the old. Music by its very nature takes hold of the passage of time and fills it with developing content. And God's Symphony is no different. Time is both tamed and celebrated as we play it. For us who have been touched by disaster that happened *at a time, or over a time, and within the physical world*, whatever the detail may have been, this physical, earthy, gritty and time-full future destiny allows us to take the substance of our particular story into the performance, with the hope that its grief and sadness will be woven into the fabric of something beautiful.

We must never lose that perspective, but we're not there yet, and we must search out where to find this God whom we forgive. Is it sufficient or satisfying enough just to cast our minds back and remember something that happened two millennia ago? Clearly not. We need God here, now. And how would this be? I suggest two answers, one a fundamental and well-known tenet of Christian belief, if that way of describing it does not devalue it; and the other something that I think is also fundamental, but often overlooked, and crucial for our healing. The first answer of course is that Christ is present with us through the Holy Spirit. 'God has given us the Spirit as a deposit, guaranteeing what is to come' (2 Cor 5:5). The presence of the Spirit was a daily reality for the first Christians, contrasting strikingly with what had been the norm for Jewish understanding, where the Spirit was more confined – either to a sense of place or to the awareness that particular individuals were identified as those upon whom the Spirit had come for a special purpose. The post-Pentecost actuality of this presence for each believer long preceded the later realisation that the Spirit could and should and must be understood as equally God with the Father and the Son. Indeed 'The more emphatic the church became that Christ was God, the more it came under pressure to clarify how Christ related to God.'[107] And to explain the conviction that Christ, though physically absent, was present with his followers. It was the pattern of God's apparent activity and presence that required an explanation, rather than being a theoretical idea that had to be forced onto the actuality of the Christians' experience. The idea of the Trinity is immensely practical, and born out of the awareness of the presence of the risen Jesus in day-to-day life. So it's clear that the first way we encounter the God whom we dare to forgive is in the person of Christ as mediated through the Holy Spirit.

But there is another way in which we can see and experience and grasp the incarnated Christ, and it is this that I want to focus on. Again, as with 'forgiving God', it may be helpful to suggest a familiar phrase but give it a new twist. So what might be new about **re-incarnation**? Well, check the spelling! This is absolutely not reincarnation, the endless return of a soul in a higher or lower order of existence, but what I can only think of calling re-incarnation – the coming again, and again and again, of Christ in the person of ordinary human beings. I can vividly remember the occasion when it first seemed to me that this was the only concept that would embrace the thought I wanted to think – and in fact the prayer that I wanted to pray. Because the daughter whose experience has been my particular starting-point for this investigation is now working and finding fulfilment as a member of the emergency services, I find I notice the work of these heroes of contemporary life

---

[107] Alister McGrath, *Christian Theology*, p 245

more consciously than before. So I was walking to work along a busy road, and saw ahead the tell-tale flashing light at the scene of an accident involving a lorry and a motorbike. It was clearly serious, and, with no practical skill to offer in the situation, I wanted to do the only thing possible, which was to pray – but in what terms? I found myself asking that the paramedics would be enabled to bring relief and healing. But that didn't seem to be quite enough to ask – or, more accurately perhaps, it didn't quite seem to do justice to their activity. I felt that my rather conventional, though I hope sincere, prayer was missing something that was happening as I walked past. Then in a rare moment of not having to think it out, I realised what that was, and that the connection was to something I had heard some months before.

Over the Christmas period, the BBC Radio 4 *Today* programme invites various well-known figures to be editor for a day, and they are encouraged to put their own stamp on the shape and content of the programmes. On Dec 28th 2004, the editor was the rock singer Bono. Well known for his support for causes and charities helping the world's poor, he specially asked for an interview to be broadcast with Sister Benedicta, a German nun who runs the Missionaries of Charity Hospital and Orphanage in Addis Ababa, Ethiopia. Her words, transcribed from the interview, were as follows:

'We will not refuse a needy person. There is an atmosphere of caring for each other. There are signs of hope, so far as people by their own suffering and by sharing the suffering of others change their approach; we call it behaviour change. We struggle with the word stigma. (HIV) Stigma can only be overcome if you come close to people who suffer. We struggle especially with [over] the children who are HIV infected. The children are innocent victims. They are all innocent victims. By coming close to people you can give hope, you can give

strength, but you, the one who goes towards suffering, you are the one who is receiving much more in human relationships, joy, satisfaction and deep happiness. This comes not from plenty, from activity, from business, from everything going well, but from the fullness of being human. You see, the people in our house have nothing left than to be human. No more health, no more work, no more family, no more money, no more riches, no more name, no more fame. They have only left to be human, very naked human. That gives a great hope.'

That is the authentic voice of Christ, re-incarnated. But there is more: in whom is it that we see Christ? Sister Benedicta is indeed bringing Christ to those who have nothing. She is being him on earth. But she acknowledges that she receives more. Jesus said, in words that have perhaps been subject to more special pleading by preachers than any other of his sayings, 'Whatever you did for one of the least of these brothers of mine, you did for me' (Matt 25:40). Let us note that 'for one of' and 'for me' must use the word 'for' in the same sense, particularly as the two phrases use the same dative case in the Greek. On its own, 'for me' could mean something like 'offered to me as an onlooker'. But clearly 'for one of the least of these my brothers' cannot contain that sense. There is only one way in which we can read the two phrases, and that is 'as service done directly to'. So in being done to them, it is done to Christ. Is he then hungry, sick or thirsty, or struggling with the stigma of HIV? Yes, he is. In being Christ to them, she meets Christ in them. This is the holy scandal of re-incarnation.

St Martin of Tours understood. Around 334, whilst serving in the Roman army, it is said that on seeing a destitute beggar he cut his cloak in half and gave it to him. He then dreamed that he met Christ wearing the cloak he had shared. Whatever we may make of the veracity of the legend, its point is clear.

The vision was not a pretty way of spiritualising an act of generosity. It was a way of understanding *what had actually happened*. The beggar was Christ.

So it was that as I walked past the scene of the accident and prayed for the injured and for those serving them, I understood that the paramedics were being Christ, and were meeting Christ. I had a glimpse of how I should pray. I had a picture of a world beginning to be filled with him, with instances of his resurrection life. If I could see the world this way, I wondered if this was perhaps a world in which I might walk with a forgiving and forgiven God.

It's worth hearing from Karl Barth again, as quoted by Roger Lundin. Barth describes Nietzsche as the one who 'was merely saying "with less restraint" and "greater honesty" what "Goethe, Hegel, Kant and Leibnitz" had long been arguing … (w)hat was it that Nietzsche … found "absolutely intolerable and unequivocally perverted" in the Christian faith? The answer, Barth says, can be discovered in his declaration of war: "Dionysus versus the Crucified." Dionysus, Zarathustra, Nietzsche himself – this was the ethical and spiritual ideal, "the lonely, noble, strong, proud, natural, healthy, wise, outstanding, splendid man." … The Christian faith sets against the Dionysian ideal what Barth calls the gospel's "blatant claim that the only true man is the man who is little, poor and sick … who is weak and not strong, who does not evoke admiration but sympathy" … Christian belief goes a step further and speaks of a crucified God; it identifies "God himself with this human type" … It places before the Olympian man the "Crucified, Jesus, as the Neighbour." '[108] And it's not just that this is

---

[108] Daniel J Treier, *The Beauty of God*, pp 202 ff, quoting Karl Barth *Church Dogmatics: the Doctrine of Creation 3/2* trans. H.Knight et al., edited by G.W. Bromiley and T.F. Torrance, Edinburgh, T&T Clark, 1960, pp 236, 232, 241

what God is like. This is where we look for him and find him.

Another example comes to mind. Helen Bamber, one of the founding members of Amnesty International, went at the age of 20 into the recently liberated Belsen concentration camp. She has said this of her contact with the survivors: *'At first I felt overwhelmed – what on earth could I do there? I used to go into these barracks and talk to people. We would sit on the floor and they would gasp out their story. It was a rasping voice, almost like a vomit, and they would vomit out their story. They would hold you, you would rock with them, and I realised after a time that there was little else I could do but to listen, to receive, because one of the problems about this kind of disaster is that we would recoil from their story. Listening, and receiving horror, was extremely important and in itself was therapeutic, because they were being believed, and I was able to say "whatever happens I will remember your story. I will be your witness. I will tell your story."* '[109] If the God whom Christ reveals is Love, then here he is.

Jürgen Moltmann's book *The Crucified God*, from which I quoted at the start of this book, is the archetypal enquiry of recent times into the subject of theodicy, in this case in particular of what that might mean after the Holocaust. Towards the end of what is a long and weighty theological argument, he draws his thoughts together into something that is deeply personal. It is significant that at this point he makes use of the writing of someone who knew Auschwitz from the inside. Speaking about the *pathos* and self-humiliation of God as seen in the Christ of the cross, Moltmann says this: 'A shattering expression of the *theologia crucis* which is suggested in the rabbinic theology of God's humiliation of himself is to be found in

---

[109] Transcribed from an interview on *Broadcasting House*, BBC Radio 4, 28th October 2007

Night, a book written by E. Wiesel, a survivor of Auschwitz:

> 'The SS hanged two Jewish men and a youth in front of
> the whole camp. The men died quickly, but the death
> throes of the youth lasted half an hour. "Where is God?
> Where is he?" someone asked behind me. As the youth
> still hung in torment in the noose after a long time, I
> heard the man call again, "Where is God now?" And I
> heard a voice in myself answer: "Where is he? He is
> here. He is hanging on the gallows …"'

Moltmann comments: 'Any other answer would be blasphemy.
There cannot be any other Christian answer to the question of
this torment. To speak here of a God who could not suffer
would make God a demon. To speak here of an absolute God
would make God an annihilating nothingness. To speak here
of an indifferent God would condemn men to indifference.'[110]
Indifferent we are not. We need to find Christ where he may be
found, and it is not where we expected.

God in Christ, having entered the auditorium and joined in
the performance of his Symphony, 'gave himself up for us'
(Eph 5:2) and in doing so lost everything, including life itself.
And we are to be 'imitators of God' (v 1) and to live this same
life of love. Christ is found again and again in the person of the
abandoned and the hopeless, and in all whom life has
wounded. He is found again and again in the person of all who
will see him in this way and who are willing to be his presence.
They, we, are called to play the music of the Prelude to Part Two
with all our hearts and with all our skill – being, and finding,
Christ in every way we can, and filling the world with instances
of his life. The music may be tragic, but the music is beautiful.

---

[110] Jürgen Moltmann, *The Crucified God*, p 283, quoting E. and M. Wiesel,
Night, Penguin Twentieth Century Classics, 2008.

At Easter 2005, BBC1 put out a play written by Rhidian Brook, entitled *Mr Harvey Lights a Candle*. I am grateful for his permission to quote from it. It told the story of a school coach trip to Salisbury Cathedral. The main protagonists were the eponymous Mr Harvey, a sad and reclusive RE teacher, played by Timothy Spall; and Helen, a beautiful but troubled teenager given to self-harm, played by Natalie Press. At the climax of the play, Mr Harvey takes the party to a particular spot in the cloisters. Suddenly finding the courage to speak of his personal life, he reveals to a stunned and for the first time respectful class that this was where he had proposed to his wife 21 years ago, and that she had committed suicide after a year of marriage. Later, he goes in search of Helen, whom he had earlier publicly berated for her personal difficulties. They finish huddled together on a walkway high up in the cathedral, where restorations are taking place. Beautiful, calm choral music can be heard from far below. The location, where something of lasting value is being restored, is surely significant as the place where the following conversation takes place.

For the first time, Mr Harvey speaks about his wife's death: 'The fact is, she chose death over life. She chose despair over hope ... She was very depressed. She thought there was nothing in the world could change how she felt ... That stuff I said about needing courage to kill yourself – it's crap. You need a lot more courage to live.' Helen asks about the music the choir are singing in the distance. 'It's about a time when God will put an end to suffering and pain, and justice will be done.' 'Do you believe all that?' she asks. 'I'm too angry to believe it,' he replies. 'Angry with who?' Mr Harvey points vaguely upward: 'With him.' Looking at her bleeding wrists, Helen says 'I'd like to believe in God and all that, but I'm too dirty.' As he replies, Mr Harvey seems to be telling Helen something he has only just seen for himself: 'That's where we find God – in the dirt. In the blood and the dirt.'

Or in the dark. No neat answers, but perhaps a language and a context. A project, a performance. Creation and re-creation. A wounded God, forgiving and forgiven. Christ made visible in acts of love. The music of the Prelude to Part Two, when every tear will be wiped away. Come, Lord Jesus.

God came in Christ to share the dark with us.

To all who need him now in this day's dark
   he comes again.
He comes again, and, soft, he comes again
Wearing the life of all who are willing
To do as he did and to share the dark.

In this way together we begin to
   make God's music.

Praying in the Dark
A Liturgy

*Faith is the aftermath of questioning – not the answers but the
quitting of doubt.*
(Lewis Hyde: *The Gift*)[111]

Spirit of Jesus, take my deepest desires, which I cannot fully
comprehend or articulate, and bring them to God for him to
deal with.

Spirit of Jesus, take my deepest fears, for which I think I have
very good grounds; take my deepest dreads which relate to
nothing specific; take even the tendency to despondency
which is built into my genes. Bring them all to God for him
to deal with.

Spirit of Jesus, keep alive in me the hope that all will be well,
and all manner of things will be well.

***

We come to God as those who wish they had not seen what
they have seen, and who wish they did not know what they
know.

Though our individual experiences are many and varied:

---

[111] Lewis Hyde, *The Gift*, first publ. Random House, 1979. Canongate
Books Ltd, 2006, p 168

We are united in bewilderment as we try to find reasons for believing that the world was created and is sustained by a loving God.

We are united in a desire not to lose faith.

We are united in a commitment to make the world better, and to be Christ in the world.

We are united in a desire not to let grief turn into bitterness.

***

May God have mercy on those whose experience of life makes it hard to believe in a God who is wise; a God who is powerful; a God who is loving.

May God sit in silence with those whose experience of life leads them to the conclusion that life is not worth living.

May God bring healing to all who are suffering at the hands of those who exercise power without justice and love.

May God come in love to those who suffer without the support of family or friends, and to those whose suffering is unknown to all, but known to God.

***

We thank God for those who have stood by us in time of need, and in whom Jesus has come to us.

May they have the patience of Christ to go on standing with us; May we have the gentleness of Christ, so that we do not make love and friendship harder for them.

We pray for those whose professional life brings them daily
into contact with grief and suffering – ministers, social
workers, counsellors, lawyers, doctors, nurses, paramedics
and many others.

Thank you for their willingness to spend their lives in support
of others.

May they be able to maintain sensitivity whilst keeping sufficient detachment to be able to help.

As they serve alongside the broken may they mirror the incarnation, life, suffering and resurrection of Christ.

So may he come and live again in his world.
So may his world be overwhelmed by love.

***

To a father in agonies of concern over his son's illness (Mk 9:23
NEB), Jesus said: 'Everything is possible to one who has faith.'

With the father we cry:
I have faith; help me where faith falls short.

BIBLIOGRAPHY

Armstrong, Karen, *The Battle for God*, Harper Perennial, 2004, p xiii ff

Barnes, Julian, *Flaubert's Parrot*, first publ. Jonathan Cape Ltd, 1984, p 147, 8

Barrow, John D., *The Artful Universe*, Penguin Books, 1995, p 38, 41

Barth, Karl, *Ethics*, New York: Seabury 1981, p 506, 507

—— *Church Dogmatics: the Doctrine of Creation 3/2*, trans H.Knight et al., ed G.W. Bromiley and T.F. Torrance, Edinburgh: T&T Clark 1960, p 236, 232, 241

Blake, William, *Songs of Innocence and Experience*, first publ 1794

Bookless, Dave, *Planetwise*, Inter-Varsity Press, 2008, p 21

Boyd, Gregory A., *God of the Possible*, Baker Books, 2000, p 90, 131

Brand, Hilary, *The Sceptic's Guide to Reading the Bible*, Bible Reading Fellowship, 2000, p 47 and elsewhere

Bryson, Bill, *A Short History of Nearly Everything*, Black Swan, 2004, p 105, 169 f, 202, 216, 573

Carroll, Lewis, *Alice's Adventures in Wonderland*, first publ. 1865, Chap. 9

Fortey, Richard, *The Earth: an Intimate History*, Harper Perennial, 2004, p 343, 349, 350

Frayn, Michael, *The Human Touch – Our part in the Creation of a Universe*, Faber and Faber, 2006, p 205

Gaarder, Jostein, *Maya*, Phoenix, 2000. Paperback 2001, p128, 278

Greene, Graham, *Travels with my Aunt*, Vintage, 1999, p 223

Gribbin, John, *Deep Simplicity*, Allen Lane, 2004. Penguin Books, 2005, p 175

Griffin, William, *C.S.Lewis, The Authentic Voice*, Lion Publishing plc, 1988, p 388

Hardy, Thomas, *The Complete Poems,* (ed. James Gibson), Palgrave Macmillan, 1991

Hopkins, Gerard Manley, *Poems and Prose*, Penguin Classics, first publ. 1953, reprinted 1987, p 50, 31

Houseman A.E., *A Shropshire Lad*, Wordsworth Editions, 1994. p 58

Hyde, Lewis, *The Gift*, first publ. Random House, 1979. Canongate Books Ltd, 2006, p 168

Lewis C.S., *The Last Battle*, first publ. Bodley Head, 1956. Puffin Books, 1971, p 50, 165

—— *The Problem of Pain*, first publ. Geoffrey Bles, 1940. Quotations from Fontana, 1959, p 83, 96

—— *A Grief Observed*, Faber and Faber, 1961. HarperCollins edition, 2001, p xx, 25

Lightman, Alan, *Einstein's Dreams*, Bloomsbury, London, 1993

Lloyd, Michael, *Café Theology*, Alpha International, 2005. Quotations from chap. 1, 2 & 3 du Maurier, Daphne, *Rebecca*, Virago Press, 2003, p 336

McGrath, Alister, *A Fine-Tuned Universe, The Quest for God in Science and Theology*,Westminster John Knox Press, 2009, p 58, 80, 69, 84 footnote, 111-114

—— *Christian Theology*, Blackwell Publishing, 2007, p 176, 177, 245

Moltmann, Jürgen, *The Crucified God*, SCM Press, first British edition 1974, third impression 2008, p261, 283

Neiman, Susan, *Evil in Modern Thought*, Princeton University Press, 2002, p 4, 5, 62

Olson, Steve, *Mapping Human History*, Bloomsbury Publishing, 2002. Paperback edition, p 34, 20

Pickover, Clifford A., *The Stars of Heaven*, Oxford University Press, 2001. Paperback 2004, p 114

[Plato, *Plato in 12 Volumes*, William Heinemann Ltd, 1966.]

Polkinghorne, John, *Exploring Reality*, Yale University Press and SPCK, 2005, p 50, 51, 58, 5f, 123, 139, 145, 181, 125

—— *The God of Hope and the End of the World*, Yale University Press and SPCK, 2002, p121, 116

—— *The Way the World Is*, first publ. Triangle, 1983. 1994, p 21, 12

Sanders, John, *The God Who Risks*, Inter-Varsity Press Academic (USA) 2nd edition, 2007, p 29, 26, 195, 196, 198, 199

Sayers, Dorothy L., *Letters of a Diminished Church*, Nashville: W Publishing, 2004, p 41

Spurling, Hilary, *Matisse the Master; a Life of Henri Matisse 1909 – 1954*, Penguin paperback, 2006. (Quoted in The Times Online book review, Jan 27th 2006)

Tennyson, Alfred, Lord, *In Memoriam A.H.H.*, first publ. 1849.

Toghill, Peter, *The Geology of Britain*, Swan Hill Press, 2000, p 83

Treier, Daniel J., Mark Husbands and Roger Lundin, *The Beauty of God. Theology and the Arts*, Intervarsity Press, 2007, p 66, 67, 207, 64, 202, 203, 204

Vanstone, W.H., *Love's Endeavour, Love's Expense*, Darton, Longman & Todd Ltd, 1977, p 47f, 53, 48

—— *The Stature of Waiting*, Darton, Longman and Todd Ltd, 1982, p ix

Wiesel, E. and M., *Night*, Penguin Twentieth Century Classics, 2008.

Wink, Walter, *Engaging the Powers*, Fortress Press, 1992, p 69, 304, 314ff

Wolterstorff, Nicholas, *Lament for a Son*, Wm.B.Eerdmans Publishing Co., 1987, p 26, 54, 97

Wordsworth, William, *Surprised by Joy*

Wright, N.T., *Evil and the Justice of God*, SPCK, 2006, p 5 footnote, 41, 67, 70.

—— *The Last Word*, HarperSanFrancisco, 2005. pp 102, 103, 104. In UK *Scripture and the Authority of God*, SPCK 2005.

Wright, Tom, *Surprised by Hope*, SPCK, 2007, p 103, 301, 305

INDEX

anthropic principle 43

Beethoven 50, 88, 139, 145

Big Bang 40, 42, 43, 47, 79, 102, 142

Brahms 155

Creationism 46, 85

cross 70, 73-75, 89, 132, 156, 161, 163, 170

Darwin. Charles 42, 45, 46, 47, 141

Dawkins, Richard 48

Deism 59, 70

Donne, John 34, 108

environment 53, 106

evolution 45-48, 67, 77, 81, 84-86, 112

Fall 57, 69-89, 113, 154

Green, Gordon 31, 88, 147

Haiti earthquake 61, 65, 105, 120

heaven 23, 46, 49, 66, 67, 123-126, 129-131, 164-165

Hubble, Edwin 41, 42

Impressionism 138-139, 142

incarnation 23, 116, 156, 158, 159, 163, 164, 166, 168

Indian Ocean tsunami 60, 62-65, 105, 120

Intelligent Design 45-47, 85

Iraq 50

Japan earthquake and tsunami 61-62, 65, 106, 120

Kant, Immanuel 51-52 (footnote), 64, 169

Leibni(t)z, Gottfried 34, 169

Lisbon earthquake and tsunami 58-60

logos 17-18, 54, 129-130, 132

Matisse, Henri 142-143, 178

Milton, John 74, 76, 79

myth/mythos 17-18, 54, 81

natural selection 45-48, 84, 141

natural theology 70

Nicea, Council of 22, 136

Nicene Creed 136

Nietzsche, Friedrich 169

open theism 49, 149

plate tectonics 62

Plato/platonic 29, 126-127, 129-130, 136

Pope, Alexander 58-59, 65-66

postmodern 9, 65, 106

resurrection 22, 53, 73-76, 87, 89, 116, 125, 128, 154, 158, 159, 164, 165, 169

Satan 109, 114-115

Shakespeare, William 118, 140

slavery 22

Stravinsky 138

Thatcher, Margaret 34

theodicy 19, 21, 34, 52, 72, 73, 84, 170

trinitarian theology 22, 70, 71

Tutu, Archbishop Desmond 23

Voltaire 59, 65, 66

Wallace, Alfred Russell 45

Williams, Rowan 161